UFOs

Other Books in the At Issue Series:

UFOs

William Dudley, *Book Editor*

David Bender, *Publisher*
Bruno Leone, *Executive Editor*

Bonnie Szumski, *Editorial Director*
David M. Haugen, *Managing Editor*

An Opposing Viewpoints® Series

Greenhaven Press, Inc.
San Diego, California

Library of Congress Cataloging-in-Publication Data

UFOs / William Dudley, book editor.
        p.   cm. — (At issue)
    Includes bibliographical references and index.
    ISBN 0-7377-0071-8 (lib. : alk. paper). —
ISBN 0-7377-0070-X (pbk. : alk. paper)
    1. Unidentified flying objects. I. Dudley, William,
1964– . II. Series: At issue (San Diego, Calif.)
TL789.U218   1999
001.942—DC21   98-55488
                                                         CIP

© 1999 by Greenhaven Press, Inc., PO Box 289009,
San Diego, CA 92198-9009

Printed in the U.S.A.

Table of Contents

Introduction

On June 24, 1947, Kenneth Arnold, a businessman and air rescue pilot, was flying his small plane over the Cascade Mountains in the state of Washington. On the lookout for a crashed airplane, he instead witnessed what he said were nine bright glistening objects flying at speeds beyond the capabilities of any known aircraft at the time. Arnold later told a reporter that the entities "flew erratic, like a saucer if you skip it across that water." Accounts of his encounter with "flying saucers" quickly spread through the news wires. Over the next several years thousands of other people reported seeing flying saucers in the skies.

The flying saucer phenomenon sparked widespread attention not only from the media and the public, but also from the U.S. government. Between 1948 and 1969, in what eventually became known as Project Blue Book, the U.S. Air Force maintained a permanent team of investigators to look into these mysterious sightings. Instead of calling the objects "flying saucers," the Air Force soon came up with the term UFOs—unidentified flying objects. Members of Project Blue Book, which included Air Force personnel and civilian scientists hired as consultants, investigated thousands of reported UFOs. Most UFO sightings were determined to have explainable causes. Some were misidentified human-made objects such as aircraft or artificial satellites. Others resulted from natural phenomena such as planets, meteors, light reflections off of clouds, flocks of birds, ball lightning, or bright stars. But investigators were unable to find explanations for 701 of the sightings, which were classified as "unidentified."

A possible explanation for these and other "unidentified" cases is what has been called the "extraterrestrial hypothesis"—the theory that some UFOs are actually spacecraft piloted by intelligent beings not of this world. This idea was voiced as early as July 4, 1947, one week after Arnold's flying saucer experience, when a news report mentioned the possibility that what the pilot saw were spaceships from other planets. It remains the most familiar and controversial explanation of UFOs. The people who investigate and write about UFOs can generally be categorized as belonging to one of two groups: those who are inclined to believe the extraterrestrial hypothesis and those who are skeptical about it. Both proponents and detractors of the theory often accuse each other of letting preconceived biases shape their examination of the available evidence.

Those who argue in favor of the extraterrestrial hypothesis argue that the universe's vast size makes life and the development of many technologically advanced civilizations highly probable. Citing the number of stars in the universe, U.S. astronaut John W. Young concluded: "If you bet against UFOs, you'd be betting against a sure thing." Supporters also point to the large number of UFO sightings (author Barry Parker writes that 100,000 incidents are on record), maintaining that they cannot *all* be dismissed as misidentified aircraft, natural phenomena, or as hoaxes. In addition to mysterious sightings, many people have claimed to have actually been abducted by aliens and taken aboard alien spacecraft. Budd Hopkins, the writer of several books on alien abduction, faults scientists for dismissing accounts of UFOs and alien abductions too easily. "Many scientists . . . maintain an interest in . . . the search for extraterrestrial intelligence," he argues. "And yet almost none of these scientists have taken the time to look into the UFO phenomena as it inarguably exists: a phenomenon consisting of tens of thousands of reports of apparent craft sightings, landings, photo and radar evidence and accounts of the temporary abduction and examination of human beings."

However, skeptics have argued that anecdotal accounts of UFO sightings and alien abductions simply do not provide enough grounds to scientifically validate the extraterrestrial hypothesis. What is needed, they say, is incontrovertible physical evidence such as undoctored photographs, debris from crashed UFOs, or other artifacts. "No good physical evidence—photographic, spectroscopic, or other—supports the hypothesis that UFOs are extraterrestrial spacecraft," writes Donald W. Goldsmith and Tobias C. Owen, authors of *The Search for Life in the Universe*. "The UFO data consist almost entirely of eyewitness accounts of things seen in the sky." Such reports are insufficient, Goldsmith and Owen contend, to support the claims that alien civilizations exist and have the means and motives to travel the extremely long distances between the stars to visit Earth. "When serious investigators who have the necessary skills examine UFO reports, they invariably find some natural cause," they argue. "Venus, meteors, falling space debris, clouds, migrating birds, airplanes, and even automobiles on elevated roadways have all been mistaken for alien spacecraft, to say nothing of deliberate hoaxes."

Some doubters of the extraterrestrial hypothesis propose another theory to explain reported UFOs and abductions. Such accounts, they assert, may instead be caused by the mental processes and spiritual needs of humans. Philosopher Paul Kurtz argues that rather than evidence of actual alien visitation, "the UFO phenomenon tells us something about the psychological and sociological behavior of the human species. . . . It is an expression of our hunger for mystery, our demand for something more, our hope for transcendental meaning." The late scientist and commentator Carl Sagan, noting the similarity of alien abduction accounts with past stories of encounters with demons, fairies and other supernatural creatures, concluded that both may be the products of the human mind. "Is it possible," he asks, "that people in all times and places occasionally experience vivid, realistic hallucinations, . . . with the details filled in by the prevailing cultural idioms?"

An important adjunct to the UFO controversy is the question of whether the U.S. Air Force and other branches of the U.S. government have lied to the American people. For believers in the extraterrestrial hypothesis, a government conspiracy to belittle UFO sightings and hide evidence of human/alien contact conveniently explains the consistent government denials concerning UFOs as well as the lack of physical evidence. A 1995 poll by Scripps-Howard News Service and Ohio University found that half of all Americans believed UFOs were alien spacecraft, and that the U.S. government was covering up knowledge of their existence. Government conspiracy theories have been harshly attacked by those who doubt the extraterrestrial hypothesis. Philip J. Klass, a UFO investigator who has written numerous books debunking claims of extraterrestrial visitation, argues that "the only credible evidence of a 'UFO coverup' that I've been able to find is by those who make such accusations against the government, and by producers of many TV shows. . . . Their false charges needlessly undermine the confidence of our own citizens in our government." Other UFO investigators, using recently declassified information, have concluded that evidence does exist of past government obstruction and deception. However, they argue that what was being covered up was not contact with aliens, but rather secret military and espionage airplanes and projects (which may themselves have caused some past UFO sightings).

More than fifty years after Kenneth Arnold's flight in the Cascades, UFOs continue to be an intriguing mystery for many Americans. People still disagree over whether accounts of UFO sightings and abductions are evidence of alien visitation, products of the human imagination, or have some other cause. The essays in *At Issue: UFOs* examine this controversy and feature the views of both supporters and doubters of the extraterrestrial hypothesis.

1

UFOs: An Overview

Charles S. Clark

Charles S. Clark is a former staff writer for CQ Researcher, *a weekly news and research report published by Congressional Quarterly Inc.*

A significant number of Americans believe that UFO sightings are caused by extraterrestrial spacecraft and that the U.S. government is hiding evidence of contact with alien civilizations. Many believe, for example, that a mysterious space vessel crashed in Roswell, New Mexico, in 1947, and that the government is secretly examining the wreckage. The U.S. government has consistently denied any cover-up. Furthermore, skeptics have voiced concern that the public fascination with UFOs signifies a disturbing rejection of science and rationality.

Forty years after seeing his first UFO, Ray Stanford still gets goosebumps telling the story: On the night of Oct. 21, 1956, he and three other teenagers in his flying saucer club were out in the salt flats near Brownsville, Texas. Suddenly, a few hundred yards away, they saw an "oblate spheroid" about 40 feet in diameter, glowing with a pulsing, electric-blue light that lit the ground.

The strange craft swooped closer—neither casting a shadow nor reflecting moonlight—and emitted an eerie hum that terrified coyotes and waterfowl. An electrostatic charge made the boys' hair stand on end; they were unable to move. The saucer landed. Then, after a few minutes, it shot straight up into the stratosphere, leaving a column of charged air and some crushed vegetation.

The experience altered Stanford's life. As an award-winning high school science student, he had been offered a scholarship to study rocket engineering at the University of Texas. Instead, he took an adult-education course in advanced physics and launched a life-long search for alien propulsion techniques far more efficient than rockets.

Investigating UFOs

Stanford eventually founded Project Starlight International, with funding from friends and a nonprofit corporation. In its heyday in Austin in the

Reprinted from Charles S. Clark, "Pursuing the Paranormal," *CQ Researcher*, March 29, 1996, by permission of Congressional Quarterly, Inc.

1970s, Starlight boasted a staff of five, including engineers and physicists who took measurements of questionable phenomena using special instruments. Their hope was to blow the scientific world wide open by proving the existence of extraterrestrial spacecraft.

"The UFO research establishment hates me because I did what they should have done," Stanford says. "They focused on tales told in the night. But I don't care how much credibility you have, human perception cannot do the job that electronic and optical equipment can do."

Today, Project Starlight has fallen on hard times. It now consists of Stanford alone and a few pieces of equipment in a spare bedroom in his modest house in College Park, Md. When he gets a chance, Stanford makes recordings of the piercing sound of magnetic waves he says are from UFOs—potential proof, he says, that aliens have mastered a unified theory of gravitational and magnetic waves that has eluded human thinkers since Einstein.

Stanford's work is familiar to Philip J. Klass, an editor at *Aviation Week & Space Technology* who has been debunking UFOs for 30 years. The two maintain cordial relations and share information on the occasional UFO hoax. "There is no credible evidence for the existence of UFOs," Klass says. "And at this point in my life, unless one landed in my front yard or on the rooftop of CNN, I would remain very skeptical. There would have to be impressive and simple evidence."

UFO enthusiasts had their eyes on Washington in 1995 when the General Accounting Office (GAO) released a report requested by Rep. Steven H. Schiff, R-N.M., seeking to answer a 50-year-old question: Is the government sitting on documents proving that a flying saucer crashed near Roswell, N.M.? The Air Force beat the GAO to the punch by releasing a phone-book-sized report with its own version of what happened.

In recent years, the estimated 19 million Americans who say they have seen a UFO have been upstaged by the 4 million people who claim, according to a 1991 Roper poll, that they were abducted by alien spacecraft. Accounts of being taken aboard, forced to undergo intimate physical examinations and even made to mate with extraterrestrials made a believer of John E. Mack, a Pulitzer Prize-winning psychiatrist whose enthusiasm sparked an alarmed review of his status on the faculty of Harvard University Medical School.

"Most of the specific information that the abductees provided about the means of transport to and from the spaceships, the descriptions of the insides of the ships themselves and the procedures carried out by the aliens during the abductions had never been written about or shown in the media," Mack wrote in his widely noted 1994 book, *Abductions: Human Encounters with Aliens.* "Furthermore, these individuals were from many parts of the country and had not communicated with each other. They seemed in other respects quite sane, had come forth reluctantly, fearing the discrediting of their stories or outright ridicule."[1]

UFOs and the paranormal

The modern debate over UFOs began raging in 1947, just after the frightening arrival of the Atomic Age. But surprisingly in the 1990s, UFOs remain a strong presence on the cultural radar screen, along with other paranormal claims—such as psychic powers, communications from ghosts and "near-death experiences."

People who claim psychic powers—and whose cable TV ads offer pay-by-the-minute services—even offer hope to police departments desperate for clues in missing-persons cases. And last November, the public learned that beginning in the early 1970s the CIA and the Pentagon had ventured into the world of the paranormal. The military and intelligence agencies had spent $20 million on Operation Stargate, a series of "remote-viewing" experiments in which psychics attempted to visualize key enemy secrets, such as whether the Soviets had developed a new submarine or whether North Korea had dug underground tunnels.

In recent years, the estimated 19 million Americans who say they have seen a UFO have been upstaged by the 4 million people who claim . . . that they were abducted by alien spacecraft.

The Internet and entertainment media offer persuasive indications that Americans are hot for the paranormal. The Net is abuzz with discussion groups reachable at the address alt.alien.visitors. Sci-fi dramas and programs reenacting the unexplained seem to dominate TV and movies. Thirty-six percent of Americans believe in ghosts, according to a 1994 Louis Harris and Associates Poll, while Gallup research reports that 8 million Americans have had a near-death experience, typically characterized by visions of being in a long, brightly lighted tunnel.

At the National Aeronautics and Space Administration (NASA), more than half of public inquiries concern UFOs, says Elsie Weigel, public information manager. Recently, "we counted 53 out of the past 139 letters forwarded to us from the White House that dealt with UFOs, and it's more if you count questions coming by phone and the Internet," she says.

Mistrust in government

Observers have noted that rising interest in UFOs coincides with high levels of mistrust in government. Stuart Vyse, a professor of psychology at Connecticut College, is preparing a survey on the two trends. "People have become so jaded and negative about government that they are willing to accept a government-conspiracy theory," he says, "which makes it easier to accept the idea of UFOs landing on Earth. Otherwise, these people reason, how would the landings go undetected?"

Conspiracy theories have long been part of the "paranormal worldview," says Paul Kurtz, chairman of the Committee for the Scientific Investigation of Claims of the Paranormal (CSICOP) and a professor of philosophy emeritus at the State University of New York at Buffalo. "Like right-wingers who fear the Trilateral Commission or the New World Order, there are people who take things that can't be explained and give them occult or mystical or spiritual overtones," Kurtz says.

Now in its 20th year, CSICOP conducts probes and publishes aggressive exposés of hoaxers and credulous people whom it believes are falling victim to a weakening of respect for science. Several outright hoaxes have been documented, among them the huge, mysterious saucer-shaped imprints found in grain fields mostly in England throughout the 1980s. Many people thought the "crop circles" were messages from alien visitors. The theory collapsed in 1991 when two British pranksters confessed to using boards to flatten the grain.[2]

In the late 1980s, purported White House documents from 1952 were made public supposedly proving that outgoing President Harry S Truman and incoming President Dwight D. Eisenhower were receiving briefings on the military's handling of 1947 UFO incidents. Klass and other skeptics used handwriting analysis and won agreement from many UFO believers that the documents were forgeries.[3]

It is clear, however, that scolding lectures from skeptics often bounce right off many who are powerfully attracted to their beliefs. "The fascination with extraterrestrials," writes *Time* magazine essayist Lance Morrow, "may reflect an exhaustion of the secrets and novelties of Earth and of earthly behavior, which, on the whole, we have come to think, is nothing to write home about. We know one another too well."[4]

The future of society's handling of the paranormal may hinge on the following questions:

Is the government covering up information on UFOs?

Veterans of the UFO debates generally fall into one of two camps, depending on their view of what took place in 1947 near Roswell Army Air Field in New Mexico. The believers' camp is certain that two flying saucers collided July 7 during a thunderstorm. They believe that a local rancher alerted personnel from the air base, who recovered unearthly debris from the crash site, including the bodies of four aliens. The base, home to the 509th Bomber Group (which had dropped atom bombs on Japan), was then the only military unit with access to atomic secrets.

Alleged coverups

Base press officer Walter Haut (who now works at a UFO museum in Roswell), put out a statement that "a flying disc" had been found. After a flurry of news reports to that effect, and after the area was closed to the public, the commander of the Eighth Air Force issued a statement explaining that what was found was a weather balloon.

It wasn't until the late 1970s that new witnesses came forward and alleged that the aliens and otherworldly debris had been transferred to Ohio's Wright-Patterson Air Force Base for secret study. One witness was Roswell mortician Glenn Dennis, who said base officials asked him for hermetically sealed caskets. At the base hospital, he said he saw strange metallic wreckage with hieroglyphic-like markings before being hustled away and threatened into silence by military police.

A nurse friend (who Dennis said later disappeared without a trace) told him she helped two doctors examine the damaged, putrid bodies of three creatures. They were "three-and-a-half to four feet tall, with disproportionately large heads. . . . The eyes were deeply set; the skulls were flexible; the nose was concave, with two orifices; the mouth was a fine slit, and the doctors said there was heavy cartilage instead of teeth. The ears were only small orifices with flaps. They had no hair, and the skin was black."[5]

Thus began the alleged coverup of what believers would call the most amazing scientific event ever. The secret supposedly would be kept by an elite group at the Pentagon, the CIA, the National Security Council and later NASA, who would pass the conspiracy down to succeeding generations.

The coverup was used again in 1952, according to assertions recently disseminated over the Internet, when sailors aboard the *USS Franklin D. Roosevelt* photographed a UFO hovering in the sky. Another coverup allegedly occurred in 1965, when a wave of flashing UFOs swarmed military facilities in California near Edwards Air Force Base. (Tapes of "panicked" radio traffic from the event can be purchased from UFO groups for $14.95.)

Surprisingly in the 1990s, UFOs remain a strong presence on the cultural radar screen.

In the late 1980s, coverup believers say astronauts aboard the space shuttle told ground controllers they had encountered strange visitors. And during the latter part of the Reagan administration, yet another coverup occurred when the Pentagon launched a top-secret "working group" to study reports of alien spacecraft, according to former *New York Times* reporter Howard Blum, who wrote a controversial book on the 40-year coverup conspiracy.[6]

Belief in such government subterfuge is broad. A July 1995 poll by the Scripps-Howard News Service and Ohio University found that 50 percent of Americans think flying saucers are real and that the government is hiding the truth about them. And it was years of pressure from the public that prompted the Air Force and GAO to produce their recent reports on the Roswell incident.

What really happened at Roswell, according to the Air Force, was recovery of debris from a top-secret radar balloon designed to measure atomic testing by the Soviet Union. Personnel at Roswell knew nothing about it because it had blown across the Sacramento Mountains from top-secret military testing facilities in Alamogordo, where tight security procedures prevented further explanation. (The radar balloon project was declassified in the 1970s.)

What makes a coverup unlikely, the Air Force adds, is that the top base commanders, by prearranged schedules, were elsewhere on the fateful day. They did not return quickly, nor did they relay any amazing news to Washington. "If some event happened that was one of the 'watershed happenings' in human history, the U.S. military certainly reacted in an unconcerned and cavalier manner," the Air Force report noted. "In an actual case, the military would have had to order thousands of soldiers and airmen, not only at Roswell but throughout the U.S., to act nonchalantly, pretend to conduct and report business as usual, and generate absolutely no paperwork of a suspicious nature."[7]

The GAO report offered both camps some ammunition. It noted that the government's own UFO investigation, which lasted from 1948–69, did not even mention a crash at Roswell in 1947. But, the GAO added, "In our search for records concerning the Roswell crash, we learned that some government records covering [air base] activities had been destroyed. The debate on what crashed at Roswell," it concluded tantalizingly, "continues."[8]

Richard Hall, chairman of the Washington, D.C.-area Fund for UFO Research, which is preparing a new report on the government's handling of UFOs, was encouraged by the GAO's intimations. The Air Force report, by contrast, "is a terrible example of overkill that is padded with irrelevant material," he says. It is designed to discourage people from plowing through its hundreds of pages to corroborate its thesis, Hall adds. "The radar balloons it speaks of were launched long after the dates in question. We consider the Roswell thing wide open, and we have hard-core evidence from witnesses whom we videotaped. Something extraordinary crashed there. We're going to keep our eye on the ball."

CSICOP's Kurtz, whose committee has examined government files and found no sign of a coverup, asks what the motive possibly would be. "Why would all the governments on the planet Earth try to withhold from citizens what would be the most important discovery of our lifetime?" he asks.

The motive, counters Hall, must be seen in the context of the Cold War. "If a UFO crashes in Roswell, the chain of command is going to ask what it all means, and they're going to try to reproduce the vehicle's power system" before our enemies do. Second, Hall says, the fear of the aliens' possible agenda would cause confusion about how best to release news of the discovery. "It could cause panic or upset whole economies," Hall says. Finally, we must remember that "the incident was handled by military, not scientific, officials, which means they may have felt the public couldn't deal with it."

Such views are seconded by Larry W. Bryant, administrator of the Alexandria, Va., group Citizens Against UFO Secrecy, which files court cases and Freedom of Information Act requests to try to expose the government's "cosmic Watergate." The alien technology would be very valuable to military planners and logistics operators, he says, but the reasons for secrecy are as much political as military.

Observers have noted that the rising interest in UFOs coincides with high levels of mistrust in government.

"My theory is that the coverup has taken on a life of its own, and that no one has the authority to let it out," he says. "There are perhaps 300 officials who handle the hard-core evidence, and there's turnover. Many have probably realized over the past 15 years that the way to handle the situation is through leaks. Roswell won't be put to rest by a report that reflects human, preconceived notions," he says of the Air Force document. "That report has logical flaws since mobile radar balloons don't carry alien bodies."

Skeptics, however, have much more to say about Roswell. Klass, who is writing a book on the subject, notes that several key witnesses to the recovery of crash debris died before there were widespread reports of unearthly remains. A key officer who was there denies any coverup.

But the politics of the issue makes it hard for authorities to put the rumors to rest categorically. "If members of Congress say there's no coverup, they make enemies," Klass says. "And if the Air Force announces that a UFO is hoax, they get criticized, so they simply say there's not enough information."

Klass has written extensively about the belief in a decades-long conspiracy to keep wraps on UFOs. In the late 1970s, for example, when the government declassified 3,000 pages on UFOs from the Pentagon, FBI, CIA and National Security Agency, officials announced that they would continue to keep 192 pages secret. UFO conspiracy theorists, of course, went haywire. But is it plausible, Klass asked, that over three decades, a coverup of the biggest secret in history would generate only six pages a year from these agencies?[9]

Klass is equally dismissive of Blum's assertion about a Pentagon UFO "working group." In a review of Blum's book, he counted 25 factual errors in a single chapter, including Blum's description of a 2,500-foot elevator shaft at a secret base in Colorado; Klass says the shaft doesn't exist.[10] Even UFO believers called the book inaccurate and overly romantic. Celebrated *New York Times* investigative reporter Seymour Hersh, whom Blum says urged him to tackle his groundbreaking project, distances himself from the book, saying its "interpretations are from Blum's own mind."

Government denials

As for the government agencies themselves, the denials are routine and longstanding. "During several space missions, NASA astronauts have reported phenomena not immediately explainable," says a space agency statement. "However, in every instance NASA determined that the observations could not be termed 'abnormal' in the space environment."

The CIA, though highly interested in UFOs in the early 1950s, has not gotten many questions in a long time, says spokesman David Christian. "We're not in the business of evaluating UFO sightings, though we have been asked to participate sometimes in review of data."

At the Defense Department, public affairs officer Maj. Tom LaRock says he is "not aware of any panel here in the building" dealing with UFOs. An Air Force boilerplate statement goes further: "Given the current environment of steadily decreasing defense budgets, it is unlikely the Air Force would become involved in such a costly project in the foreseeable future."

Barry Bitzer, press secretary for Rep. Schiff, explains that Schiff requested the GAO report on Roswell after pressure from citizens and after he "got the runaround from [the] Pentagon, which simply told him to go to the National Archives. The intention was to make the issue open and accessible, and we are satisfied that the GAO did what it could under the restraints of time," Bitzer says. "The original Air Force answer about a weather balloon didn't wash because you don't seal off an area for a weather balloon. When government is unnecessarily secretive, it fosters this kind of conspiracy theory. Now people can draw their own conclusions."

Questioning science

Is respect for the scientific method in danger?

"You're more alive after death than at any time since you were last born," writes P.M.H. Atwater, describing her three experiences of nearly dying and then returning to life. The sensation is different "because you no longer wear a dense body to filter and amplify the various sensations you had once regarded as the only valid indicators of what constitutes life."[11]

The writer's reliance on personal testimony, bathed in warm, spiritual language devoid of skeptical tones, is common to many who embrace the paranormal. The style permeates the alien-abduction claims discussed by Mack, who writes: "As we suspend the notion of our preeminent and dominating intelligence, we might open to a universe filled with life forms different from ourselves to whom we might be connected in ways we do not yet understand."[12]

---

50 percent of Americans think flying saucers are real and that the government is hiding the truth about them.

To skeptics, such approaches are a worrisome trend. And the skeptics are getting organized. In June 1995, the New York Academy of Sciences assembled 200 scientists, physicians, philosophers and educators to its "Flight from Science and Reason" conference.

CSICOP's Kurtz, who addressed the gathering, asks with frustration, "How is the ordinary person to distinguish reality from fiction? If someone says he saw a poltergeist or a spaceship in his backyard, he never hears any criticism. There's a Hallelujah chorus around near-death experiences. The claims are not corroborated or tested. It's very troubling. If a patient tells you he's Bismarck or Napolean, you'd say he's delusional. But John Mack is taking the reports from patients as true."

Kurtz worries that people concentrate on supposed "creatures who are more intelligent and technologically advanced than us and wonder whether they are benevolent or malevolent. The creatures are said to deliver some profound messages, such as 'Be peaceful' or 'Save the environment.' It's really a post-modern symbol of divine revelation. And because of the will to believe, people get angry when we skeptics come in."

Fascination with the paranormal

Carl Sagan, the famed Cornell University astronomer, blasts the current fascination with the paranormal in his 1995 book, *The Demon-Haunted World.* "Superstition and pseudoscience keep getting in the way" of scientific truth, he writes, "distracting us, providing easy answers, dodging skeptical inquiry, casually pressing our awe buttons and cheapening the experience, making us routine and comfortable practitioners as well as victims of credulity."[13]

Part of the skeptics' complaint is that the books, articles and television programs that meet their standards enjoy nowhere near the drawing power of those that circulate strange claims. Leon Jaroff, a long-time *Time* magazine writer who wrote the "Skeptical Eye" column for *Discover* magazine, complains that on *Time*'s new Internet venture, the most popular category of highlights from the magazine is not national news or the arts but a feature called "alien ruins on the moon."

"Most people are so desperate to believe that they lose all sense of rationality or objectivity," he says. "I say, why not look at the magic around you, look what you can do with your computer, look at the search for new planets. But it's not enough. People have got to have their neighbors being kidnapped and sexually examined by aliens."

One reason that many people reject science, writes mathematician John Allen Paulos, is that "New Age" beliefs in astrology, biorhythms or Tarot cards comfort them by offering "personally customized pronouncements."[14] Such people shy away from cold and impersonal scientific questions—How long? How fast? Which is more likely?

Psychology Professor Vyse points out that science does offer explanations for most strange phenomena. People who recount near-death experiences, for example, seem to have already known about such common details as the "tunnel of light. So, not surprisingly, they report what they're supposed to report," he says. "There's also the possibility that a physiological process could stimulate such experiences, such as neurological damage."

Paranormal enthusiasts, however, often reject the traditional church, science and medical establishments, preferring to revel in "the culture of the moment," Vyse says. "There is an excitement to being the individual who has sighted something unique and special. It is similar to religion. I used to think that education levels mattered when it came to such behavior. But now I see that certain people are simply brought up in social groups where it is accepted. Superstitions are common among college students, for instance. Harvard students still rub the foot of the statue of John Harvard on the day of an exam."

Many UFO researchers distinguish between mere claims and scientific empiricism.

Many observers note that education can only go so far. Gerald Weissmann, a doctor at New York University Medical Center, told the June conference to consider Russia and France. "Both countries educate their young people in science far better than we do. But the belief in magic and the supernatural is certainly more widespread in France and Russia than it is in the United States."[15]

What's more, among explorers of the paranormal, there has long been frustration with scientists who come across as arrogant. As far back as 1961, a Brookings Institution report on the possibility of other life in outer space contained the following comment: "It has been speculated that of all groups, scientists and engineers might be the most devastated by the discovery of relatively superior creatures, since these professions are most clearly associated with the mastery of nature, rather than with the understanding and expression of man."[16]

Laurence W. Frederick, an astronomer at the University of Virginia who helps run the Society for Scientific Exploration, a paranormal investigative group, says: "There are dogmatists on one side, mostly scientists, who won't even think about the possibility that something about the paranormal might be real. But I point to the many times scientists have overlooked things that later became dogma. Stones coming out of the sky were long said by scientists to be the result of lightning hitting rocks. But in 1804, they were identified as meteors after chemical analysis showed they were extraterrestrial."

Frederick says he knows scientists at universities who believe in reincarnation and in the Loch Ness monster. But his group's only requirement is that researchers keep an open mind. "People who present evidence to us know that they have to make a good case. Sometimes we say these things are crazy, other times we say they make a little sense. But the skeptical approach taken by CSICOP is too one-sided," he adds. If something from the paranormal is eventually proved, "They will look bad."

Many UFO researchers distinguish between mere claims and scientific empiricism. As the Chicago-based J. Allen Hynek Center for UFO Research notes in a pamphlet, "the majority of sightings generally prove to be a misinterpretation of natural phenomena—meteors, planets, stars, odd clouds—or manmade objects, such as airplanes, balloons or satellites. Smaller number of reports cannot be investigated properly for various reasons—lack of pertinent details, for example, or inaccessibility of witnesses. However, in any given number of UFO reports, about 5 percent to 10 percent are truly puzzling. . . . These cases are considered true UFO reports."

Hall of the Fund for UFO Research, who earned a philosophy degree studying the scientific method, says he is "involved in gathering data and not pushing a theory. There are lots out there that need study, but it's not being recognized as a genuine problem, partly because CSICOP debunks it," he says. He recommends more research into data from radar sightings of UFOs; more studies on the effects of electromagnetism on cars, trucks, airplanes, animals and humans (a common detail reported in UFO sightings); and more analysis of films and photos of UFOs.

Such research, not surprisingly, does not seem pressing to skeptic Klass. "One of the important fingerprints in deciding whether something is protoscience or pseudoscience," he says, "is that the passage of time provides more evidence either to enhance or discredit a theory. Today we don't know one iota more about UFOs than we knew 40 years ago."

Historical background

Sightings of objects in the sky go back to biblical times, to the Books of Ezekiel and Exodus. That the concept has carried through the centuries is evidenced by Christian paintings of the Middle Ages, which portray prophets ascending to heaven in what at least in one case looks like an egg-shaped metallic vehicle.[17]

But the modern clash between the public's appetite for the eerie and the hard-won authority of science has its roots in the 19th century. It was in 1848 in upstate New York that two young girls who were said to communicate with the dead helped to launch the wave of spiritualism that swept the country. Hundreds visited Katie and Margaret Fox in their parlor to hear spooky, rapping noises in the dark. Believers included Abraham Lincoln, Susan B. Anthony, Horace Greeley, P.T. Barnum and Frederick Douglass. Eventually, the writer and psychologist William James became president of a group called the American Psychical Society, while the Society for Psychical Research arose in London.

Nathaniel P. Tallmadge, D-N.Y., a U.S. senator and later governor of the Wisconsin territory in the 1840s, led a drive that gathered 15,000 names on a petition to push Congress to fund a scientific study of the powers of so-called mediums. Congress declined, however, and Katie and Margaret were eventually exposed as phonies. They had made the rapping sounds by cracking their toe joints.[18]

Americans' interest in the fantastic offered an enthusiastic reception to a 1882 book by former Rep. Ignatius Donnelly, R-Minn., boosting belief in the lost island of Atlantis. And several years before the Wright brothers took flight—when lighter-than-air craft were quaintly called "air ships"—sightings were reported across 19 states during a six-month period. In 1897, a "cigar-shaped object 300 feet long made of panels of glass" was reported by a Kansas farmer who, with his son, swore that "six of the strangest beings I ever saw" extended a red cable down from their vehicle and grabbed up one of his cows.[19]

The term "flying saucer" entered the national lexicon in 1947.

One of the first people to suggest that UFOs were alien visitors was New Yorker Charles Hoy Fort. In 1919, after years of study at the New York Public Library and the British Museum, he published his *Book of the Damned* (recently republished) that encouraged study of paranormal phenomena. "Fort was skeptical about scientific explanations, observing how scientists argued according to their beliefs, rather than the rules of evidence, and that inconvenient data was ignored," says the London-based *Fortean Times,* which carries on Fort's tradition today, along with the Arlington, Va.-based International Fortean Organization.

It was in the 1920s that a psychologist named J.B. Rhine took up a post at Duke University, creating the first academic program in "parapsychology." He would become famous for coining the term "extrasensory perception" (ESP) and for experiments in which blindfolded subjects reportedly identified playing cards as many as 25 times in a row.

The age of UFOs

The public had had two years to adjust to the existence of weapons of mass destruction when the era of UFOs dawned. The term "flying saucer" entered the national lexicon in 1947—two years after atomic bombs had been dropped on Hiroshima and Nagasaki. Pilot Kenneth Arnold reported seeing UFOs travelling 1,000 mph above Mt. Rainier, Wash. They resembled "a saucer skipping over water," he noted in the inaugural issue of *Fate* magazine, still published in St. Paul, Minn.

Though some 853 UFO sightings were recorded in 1947, a Gallup Poll showed that only 1 percent of Americans felt flying saucers made an important news story that year (23 percent cited instead the high cost of living). By 1950, however, 47 percent believed in UFOs, nearly the same percentage as today.

The government, deep into the Cold War in the 1950s and operating on a war footing for the Korean conflict, denied public charges that it was hiding UFO evidence. In fact, the Air Force in 1948 had launched Project Grudge, a highly classified group headed by California Institute of Technology physicist H.P. Robertson, to study the phenomenon. In 1952—the year of a record 1,501 UFO sightings—the inquiry (by then renamed Blue Book) reported to U.S. intelligence and military authorities that it had no evidence that UFOs were extraterrestrial. As sightings continued over the next dozen years, Congress consulted occasionally with the Air Force concerning UFOs, and private citizens formed their own investigative groups.

UFOs on Capitol Hill

In March 1966, Michigan congressman (and future president) Gerald R. Ford wrote to Armed Services Committee Chairman Mendel Rivers, D-S.C.: "In the firm belief that the American public deserves a better explanation than that thus far given by the Air Force, I strongly recommend that there be a committee investigation of the UFO phenomena."[20]

The following week, Rivers' committee took testimony from Air Force Secretary Harold Brown and Air Force consultant J. Allen Hynek, an astronomer then at Ohio State University. Brown said he knew of no one with scientific or executive standing in the Air Force who thought that UFOs were extraterrestrial. But Hynek said he knew of 20 UFO cases that needed further study and recommended creation of a civilian panel. One committee member, Rep. Felix Hebert, D-La., asked Hynek whether he'd conferred with Ray Walston, the actor then playing a Martian on a popular TV show.

Two years later, however, the topic was accorded more respectful treatment at a symposium on UFOs sponsored by the House Science and Astronautics Committee. This time no one from the Air Force appeared. Hynek testified as a private citizen, and pro-UFO meteorologist James E. McDonald was brought in with five other experts who called for more research on the topic.

McDonald said he took very seriously the possibility that UFOs are extraterrestrial and warned that witnesses were reluctant to come forward for fear of ridicule. University of Illinois sociologist Robert Hall, brother of Richard Hall, testified that while some UFOs may result from "hysterical contagion," there were hard-core cases that didn't lend themselves to that interpretation. Written testimony presented to the committee speculated on a link between UFO sightings and ESP. Even astronomer Sagan, though the only witness expressing skepticism toward flying saucers, recommended that the government fund research into life elsewhere in the universe.[21]

The symposium's chairman, Rep. J. Edward Roush, D-Ind., said that while the panel would take no stand on UFOs, "Events of the last half-century certainly verify the American philosopher John Dewey's conclusion that 'every great advance in science has issued from a new audacity of the imagination.'" (Roush was defeated for re-election in 1968 and went on to join a UFO group.)

By the end of the 1960s, the Air Force had decided to get out of UFO investigations. It shut down Project Blue Book at Wright-Patterson Air Force Base, reporting that it had studied 12,618 sightings, and that only 701 remained "unidentified." The Air Force decision was based on the so-called Condon Report, after University of Colorado physicist Edward U. Condon. The report, "Scientific Study of Unidentified Flying Objects," concluded that further government study of UFOs was unlikely to advance science.

Although the report, released as a commercial paperback, hedged its bets by recommending that private groups continue the search, UFO enthusiasts protested loudly, calling it a political document unrepresentative of advanced science and even a CIA plot. "Had I known of the extent of the emotional commitment of the UFO believers and the extremes of conduct to which their faith can lead them," Condon wrote, "I certainly would never have undertaken the study."[22]

The 1970s were still young when UFO sightings began grabbing headlines anew. Dramatic testimony, such as the claim by two Mississippi fishermen that they had been taken aboard a spacecraft, prompted astronomer Hynek, then at Northwestern University, to switch to the pro-UFO camp and start his Center for UFO Studies. (It was Hynek who formulated the hierarchy of UFO encounters popularized by Steven Spielberg's 1977 movie "Close Encounters of the Third Kind.")

Rumors of a government coverup persisted, and more amateur investigators took to the field with ever more complicated theories. On Indian reservations near Yakima, Wash., forest-fire lookouts began reporting orange-red balls and "deep rumbling noises." After years of investigation, researcher Greg Long of Philomath, Ore., wrote: "I toss out this idea as a wild idea—the orange spheres are an intelligence, capable of knowing the work of UFO researchers and of appearing in faulted, earthquake-prone areas during periods of tectonic strain buildup and release, as a red herring, while other UFOs carry out their operations."[23]

In 1977, Jimmy Carter assumed the presidency and followed through on a subject that had interested him since 1969, when he had seen and reported a UFO. (One investigator concluded that what Carter saw was the planet Venus.) Carter asked NASA Administrator Robert A. Frosch to consider conducting new research on UFOs. The NASA chief respectfully declined, citing "an absence of tangible or physical evidence available for thorough laboratory analysis."[24]

By this time, the UFO issue was of international concern. In 1977, Sir Eric Gairy, prime minister of Grenada, addressed the United Nations about his own sighting. And in 1990, Belgium became the first government to openly investigate UFOs after a series of sightings.

Remote viewing

In November 1995, many Americans were startled to read that the government was discontinuing a program that most never even knew about. Intermittently since the early 1970s, the CIA and the Defense Department had spent some $20 million on research into a paranormal technique called "remote viewing." The program at Fort Meade, Md., and the Stanford Research Institute in Palo Alto, Calif., was designed to test whether people with the supposed paranormal power known as *psi* could provide otherwise unobtainable military data.

For years, the government kept several "psychics" on the payroll who were available for use by federal agencies. One of them, a former Army intelligence officer named Joe McMoneagle, won a decoration for pinpointing the location of a new Soviet submarine. He now offers his services as a psychic in Nellysford, Va., charging clients $1,500 a day.[25]

The Pentagon's decision to halt the remote-viewing program came after a consulting firm evaluated all recent research into psychic phenomena. The evaluation focused on experiments such as those in which subjects stared at *National Geographic* magazine photographs and attempted to send mental pictures of what they were looking at to psychics at other locations, who would then attempt to draw the same pictures. University of Oregon psychologist Ray Hyman was more skeptical than his co-evaluator Jessica Utts, a statistician at the University of California at Davis.

> *In 1990, Belgium became the first government to openly investigate UFOs after a series of sightings.*

"Parapsychology, unlike the other sciences, has a shifting data base," Hyman wrote in rejecting remote viewing. "Experimental data that one generation puts forth as rock-solid evidence for psi is discarded by later generations in favor of new data."

Replied Utts: "I have never seen a skeptic attempt to perform an experiment with enough trials to even come close to insuring success." The consulting firm's conclusion, however, was that "evidence for the operational value of remote viewing is not available."[26]

For years, support for the remote-viewing project had come from Rep. Charlie Rose, D-N.C., and Sen. Claiborne Pell, D-R.I., a well-known paranormal enthusiast.[27] Pell sits on the boards of paranormal research groups—and has debated the merits of psychic phenomena with magician James "The Amazing" Randi, who now devotes his time to debunking psychics as charlatans. "I have long been interested in psychic phenomena, including the area of 'remote viewing,' as legitimate areas for scientific inquiry and possible practical applications," Pell said recently. "If the CIA is not interested, that's their business. I am convinced, however, that we should continue to research these and other areas that have the potential of improving the human condition."

Police and psychics

Increasingly in recent years, news media accounts of crime investigations have noted that police have consulted "psychics." Frustrated officers in Montgomery County, Md., in 1992 followed leads provided by psychics to try to find the body of Laura Houghteling, a 23-year-old woman later found to have been murdered. And the family of Polly Klaas, the young girl kidnapped and murdered in Petaluma, Calif., in 1993, accepted help from psychics during a manhunt. Her grieving father, however, later denounced them as "predators."[28]

More recently, CSICOP members joined with station WCAU-TV in Philadelphia to unmask people who offer psychic services to crime victims. They concocted a story about a missing girl and then released the "details" of her life. A hundred people claiming to be psychics called the father with "insights" into her condition and whereabouts, but none figured out that she wasn't really missing.[29]

"Some police departments turn to psychics as facilitators when they run out of clues, or to show families that all possible leads are being followed," says Hubert Williams, president of the Police Foundation. "It's controversial in the law enforcement community. Some say it is not sufficiently scientific; others say they are getting good results."

Maggie Blackman, director of public relations at the Institute for Parapsychology, in Durham, N.C., says that many police departments use psychics but don't make the practice public, vaguely crediting any information they receive from psychics to "a source." "Some information [they receive] helps a case, and some doesn't," she says. *"Psi* scientists believe everyone is born with some *psi,* just as we can all draw and sing," Blackman explains. "But are we all artists and singers? Real psychics can't turn *psi* on and off like a faucet. They can have a bad day and bomb in the laboratory."

The institute, the off-campus successor to the original Rhine project at Duke, continues research into telepathy, clairvoyance and psychokinesis. Recent media exposés of phony psychics who work through 900 phone numbers and bilk people of their life savings are helping preserve her group's scientific dignity, Blackman says. "We're looking at what situations are conducive to having *psi* happen—your mood, the weather, the geomagnetic field. We'll never figure it out completely, but we can figure to what extent it's applicable."

The true believers

When the Air Force receives calls about UFOs, it refers them to the many private interest groups listed in Gale's *Encyclopedia of Associations.* Recently three of the biggest UFO groups formed a partnership to foster more cooperation, with one-shot funding from Las Vegas developer Robert T. Bigelow. The Fund for UFO Research has raised more than $500,000 and awarded 30 research grants. The Seguin, Texas-based Mutual UFO Network holds conferences and coordinates an amateur radio network. The Center for UFO Studies in Chicago takes telephoned reports of sightings and investigates those that look promising.

In Yucca Valley, Calif., Gabriel Green, the longtime head of the Amalgamated Flying Saucer Clubs of America and a former U.S. presidential candidate, recently sent out word in his newsletter that UFOs and government coverups will dominate this year's national elections. Moreover, he said that the Japanese government is threatening to release extensive UFO files if the U.S. government doesn't release its own.

Ed Komarek, co-founder of the Gaithersburg, Md., UFO group Operation Right to Know, is running for Congress. "The coverup of the reality of advanced space-faring civilizations coming to us from space by world governments is contributing to the stagnation and devolution of world societies," his campaign literature warns.

In the scientific realm, the Enterprise Mission, an investigative group in Weehawken, N.J., continues publishing and lecturing on an alleged NASA coverup of photographic evidence purportedly showing artificial structures on the moon. Believers say the huge, glass structures display advanced architectural techniques from a long-lost civilization. The group (formerly the Mars Mission) contends that films and photographs taken by Apollo astronauts are mysteriously missing from NASA's public offerings.

Other active paranormal groups include the Ancient Astronaut Society, of Highland Park, Ill., which claims members in 93 countries. It leads its members on expeditions to explore land formations and mysterious sculptures thought to be the work of aliens. The International Association for Near-Death Studies in East Windsor Hill, Conn., promotes research and publishes journals. And the Annapolis, Md.-based American Association of Electronic Voice Phenomena, with 250 members in 39 states, circulates cassette tape recordings of what it says are the voices of ghosts.

> *Some scholars . . . suggest that UFO . . . phenomena may represent something beyond the either-or choices of literal truth and pure fiction.*

Interest in the paranormal continues as a boost for tourism. The UFO museum in Roswell offers a bronze medallion commemorating the 1947 "incident" to donors of $25. And 85 miles north of Las Vegas, the state of Nevada last winter spent $3,300 putting up signs proclaiming the "extraterrestrial highway." The region has a reputation for mystery because it is home to Area 51, a top-secret Defense Department facility thought to test special aircraft. Tiny Gulf Breeze, Fla., meanwhile, enjoys a reputation among cognoscenti as the "UFO capital of the United States."

But the skeptics are gearing up to respond to the continued activism. To mark its 20th anniversary, CSICOP is planning nothing less than "The First World Skeptics Congress," to be held in June 1996 in Buffalo, N.Y. The three-day conference, titled "Science in the Age of (Mis)Information," will feature numerous writers and scientists of note, including writer and zoologist Stephen Jay Gould of Harvard, who will deliver the keynote address.

The outlook for UFOs

People who claim to have been abducted by aliens are not mentally ill, according to a team of psychologists at Carleton University in Ottawa, Canada, who conducted a battery of tests on such subjects in 1993. "They tend to be white-collar, relatively well-educated representatives of the middle class," they reported. However, the study also noted that 80 percent of the alleged abductions took place at night, 60 percent of them while the subject was asleep.[30]

Some scholars, among them University of Connecticut psychologist Kenneth Ring, suggest that UFO and near-death phenomena may represent something beyond the either-or choices of literal truth and pure fiction. "Perhaps there is, after all, a third realm of the imagination in its own right," he writes, "not as something unreal, but as something objectively self-existent, the cumulative product of imaginative thought itself."[31]

But CSICOP's Kurtz points out that most academic experts are skeptical of colleagues who get involved in the paranormal. "Hynek was virtually the only astronomer defending close encounters," he says, "yet a small fringe can get all the attention."

Many scholars are reluctant to criticize their peers, notes Terence J. Sandbek, a Sacramento, Calif., psychologist. "They feel uncomfortable in the public limelight; they don't want to be seen as a negative person; still others see the whole issue as so silly as to not deserve a response."[32]

Skeptic Klass, who has collected many times on his longstanding bet that no one can present proof of UFOs, is a familiar fixture at UFO conferences. He is treated amicably, even though the Mutual UFO Network sells dartboards bearing his likeness.

"The vast majority of UFO believers are not in it for the money—they fund many of their own investigations," he says. "But notice that none of these people who claim to have been abducted by UFOs has produced one iota of new scientific evidence. You might expect if these aliens are so wise, they would quickly give us a cure for AIDS or point to a place in the sky where we might discover a new planet."

Hall of the Fund for UFO Research finds Klass "intellectually dishonest. When you pin him down on one point, he makes a joke and won't debate."

Members of CSICOP do worry that their skepticism may come across as harsh. "We must be fair-minded and objective," says Kurtz. "But at some point, we become exasperated, and we have to debunk to keep alive an appreciation for the reflective mind." The United States is "the most advanced technological culture in the world," he adds. "A failure to appreciate the scientific method will undermine our power in the world, our responsibility and our future."

The search goes on

Meanwhile, Stanford keeps up his searching, sometimes using computer-enhanced images of UFOs captured on film. One photo that he says he took at an altitude of 39,000 feet—while on a Braniff Airlines flight in 1977—shows beams of plasma (hot ionized gas) emanating from a UFO. This is another sign, he says, of an alien technology that permits a craft to move at extraordinary speed.

"Whichever nation gets the secret to this could rule the world," Stanford says. "As a youth, I was naive in thinking that I could simply prove this with instruments," and then the U.S. government would reveal its secrets. "But now I see that the government has its hands on an incredibly complex problem, a legitimate intelligence issue. It has to protect potential breakthroughs from being leaked to our enemies."

Notes

1. John E. Mack, M.D., *Abductions: Human Encounters with Aliens* (1994), p. 1.

2. *Skeptical Inquirer*, May 1995, p. 41, published by the Committee for the Scientific Investigation of Claims of the Paranormal (CSICOP).

3. Timothy Good, *Alien Contact: Top Secret UFO Files Revealed* (1993), p. 123.

4. *Time*, Feb. 5, 1996, p. 51.

5. Karl T. Pflock, "'Project Snafu' and the Real Secret of Roswell," Fund for UFO Research, Issue paper No. 1, 1994, p. 59.

26   *At Issue*

6. Howard Blum, *Out There: The Government's Secret Quest for Extraterrestrials* (1990), p. 40.

7. Headquarters United States Air Force, *The Roswell Report: Fact Versus Fiction in the New Mexico Desert*, 1995, p. 3.

8. General Accounting Office, *Government Records: Results of a Search for Records Concerning the 1947 Crash Near Roswell, N.M.*, July 1995.

9. Philip J. Klass, *UFOs: The Public Deceived* (1983), p. 50.

10. Philip J. Klass, "Did the U.S. government set up a top secret UFO Working Group?" Book review of *Out There: The Government's Secret Quest for Extraterrestrials*, in *Scientific American*, February 1991, p. 140.

11. P.M.H. Atwater, *Beyond the Light: What Isn't Being Said About Near-Death Experience* (1994), p. 182.

12. Mack, *op. cit.*, p. 422.

13. Carl Sagan, *The Demon-Haunted World: Science As a Candle in the Dark* (1996), as excerpted in *Skeptical Inquirer*, March-April 1996, p. 28.

14. Quoted in Terence J. Sandbek, "Hungry People Who Buy Imaginary Food with Real Money: Psychology, Mysticism, Superstition and the Paranormal," paper at the American Psychological Association convention, Aug. 17, 1991.

15. Quoted in Malcolm W. Browne, "Scientists Deplore Flight From Reason," *The New York Times*, June 6, 1995, p. C1.

16. Quoted in Michael Zimmerman, "Why Establishment Leaders Resist the Very Idea of Superior Non-Human Intelligence," Fund for UFO Research, Issue Paper No. 1. The Brookings Institution report, "Proposed Studies on the Implications of Peaceful Space Activities for Human Affairs," was prepared for the National Aeronautics and Space Administration and distributed by the House Committee on Science and Astronautics, April 18, 1961.

17. Editors of Time-Life Books, *The UFO Phenomenon* (1987), p. 17.

18. From the PBS documentary "Telegrams from the Dead," *The American Experience*, broadcast Oct. 19, 1994.

19. Marcia S. Smith, "The UFO Enigma," Congressional Research Service, June 20, 1983, p. 47.

20. Timothy Good, *Above Top Secret* (1988), p. 260.

21. Symposium on Unidentified Flying Objects: Hearings before the House Committee on Science and Astronautics, July 29, 1968.

22. Cited in Smith, *op. cit.*, p. 75.

23. *MUFON UFO Journal*, June 1990, p. 6.

24. Quoted in C.B. Scott Jones, "Myth, Reality and Misinformation About Government Secrecy," Issue Paper No. 1, Fund for UFO Research, 1994, p. 1.

25. *The Washington Post*, Nov. 30, 1995.

26. Quoted in Michael D. Mumford, Andrew M. Rose and David A. Goslin, "An Evaluation of Remote Viewing: Research and Applications," American Institutes for Research, Sept. 29, 1995.

27. Quoted in Martin Gardner, "The Senator from Outer Space," *Skeptical Inquirer*, March-April 1996, p. 12.

28. Quoted in *The Washington Post,* March 10, 1994.

29. *Skeptical Inquirer,* November-December 1995, p. 6.

30. The Associated Press, Nov. 1, 1993.

31. Kenneth Ring, *The Omega Project: Near-Death Experiences, UFO Encounters and Mind at Large* (1992), p. 218.

32. Sandbek, *op. cit.*

2

Extraterrestrial Spacecraft Are Real

Chris W. Brethwaite

Chris W. Brethwaite is a writer and a former radar operator with the Air National Guard.

The author recounts his encounters with UFOs, which include both visual sightings and mysterious radar signals. Witnessing a UFO that cannot be explained was for him a profound and unforgettable event. Such experiences caused him to realize that humanity is not alone in the universe.

Thanks to my dad I've been interested in UFOs since I was 10. In the early 1950s, when he was an air force officer, pilots told him of strange encounters with disc-shaped objects that outperformed their jets. Later, he shared these tales with me, and still later, I had my own encounters with UFOs.

In 1976, I was living in Phoenix, Arizona, and in addition to my full-time job, I was a radar operator in the Air National Guard. That February, my outfit, a mobile radar unit, packed up and headed for China Lake Naval Weapons Center in California for two weeks of annual training.

We set up our radar on top of Straw Peak, a mountain 40 miles east of Ridgecrest, California, that overlooked the test range. It was a desolate area, far removed from civilization. From our vantage point, you could see over 100 miles in all directions.

One night, another radar operator and I were assigned the graveyard shift. Since there weren't any training exercises scheduled, we took turns manning the scope. I was at my console trying to get some shut-eye when my partner yelled, "Hey, take a look at this!" I sat up and looked at my screen. Sure enough, there was an unknown about 50 miles out, flying right for us. Normally this wouldn't have caused concern, but the airspace around us was off limits to all aircraft except military craft.

I calculated the object's speed at 700 mph and then turned on the SIF—the Selective Identification Feature. What I was doing was asking my radar to identify the plane by processing the signal sent out by its

Reprinted from Chris W. Brethwaite, "They Came from Outer Space," *Fate*, September 1995, by permission of *Fate* magazine. Copyright ©1995 Llewellyn Worldwide, Ltd.

transponder. To my surprise there was no response. My radar screen continued painting a raw target. The object kept coming toward us, though every once in a while it would disappear from the screen for a moment or two. Most likely whatever it was it was hugging the terrain and we were losing it behind hills and buttes.

When the object got right on top of us, I ran outside to see if I could spot it. It was a perfectly clear night, but I couldn't see anything in the sky, so I went back inside. Radar now showed that the object was outbound, going back the same direction it had come from—in the general direction, I now realize, of the Nellis Test Range, home of Area 51 [a secret military base in Nevada]. We tracked it until it was no longer within range of our equipment.

The next morning, I mentioned the sighting to my CO, Captain Steve Hepburn, and discovered that he had had a visual sighting of a UFO a day or two prior to our radar sighting.

He had come out of the radar hut early one morning and had seen a red, glowing orb hanging motionless in the sky not far from our position. He was reluctant to discuss his sighting with me. I presume it was because he didn't want to be associated with anything that could hinder his chances for advancement. Consequently, I know nothing more about his sighting.

A return visit

Ironically, UFOs made a return visit the following year during our summer camp. Once again we went to California, this time to a mountaintop outside of Big Bear City in the San Bernardino National Forest. As always, our radar was on top of the mountain, our base camp was halfway up the mountain, and we had a security checkpoint at the base of the slope.

It was after sunset. Several of my fellow guardsmen and I were at the checkpoint waiting for a truck to take us to base camp. I was standing in a clearing talking to one of the sky cops. To my left, about 20 degrees above the horizon, was a bright light which I took to be Venus or some bright star. About 20 minutes into our conversation, this light started moving. The sky cop and I both noticed this, and since neither of us knew what it was, he went to his jeep and got a pair of binoculars.

To the naked eye the object appeared to be nothing more than a ball of white light. But through the binoculars, it looked to be a glowing orange triangle in an upright position with numerous multi-colored lights. We pointed out the object to the other people there, and they too looked at it through the binoculars. Nobody had any idea what it was.

There are times when I wish that I could forget all about UFOs and aliens, but I can't.

For the next 15 minutes it flew an elliptical pattern, in toward us and then back out. The closest it got to us was about three miles. Somebody in our group called up the hill to see if we had it on radar, but our equipment was down for repairs.

Several nights after this sighting, a fellow radar operator, Denzil Solo-man, left his tent late one night to use the latrine. He saw a light streak across the sky, stop dead in the air, and take off again at high speed.

There are times when I wish that I could forget all about UFOs and aliens, but I can't. Seeing a non-human entity is a profound experience, one that stays with you for your entire life. Because of these experiences, I know that we are not alone in this universe, and for reasons I don't fully understand, I feel compelled to share this truth with others. Perhaps it's because confession is good for the soul. In any event, life goes on. Here and on other planets.

3

Extraterrestrial Spacecraft Crashed at Roswell, New Mexico, in 1947

Jim Marrs

Jim Marrs, a journalist and UFO researcher, is author of Alien Agenda: Investigating the Extraterrestrial Presence Among Us.

A controversial object crashed close by Roswell, New Mexico, in July 1947. Debris found by a rancher was soon removed by U.S. military units. The U.S. government, which initially claimed that the discovered wreckage was a weather balloon, now argues that it was from a secret military balloon. However, the government's past record of lies and deceit casts doubt on its story. A more likely explanation, supported by many witnesses that have come forward, is that the U.S. military recovered debris from a crashed alien spaceship.

No UFO story has captured the imagination of the public as has the reported crash at Roswell, New Mexico. It remains one of the most well documented of UFO issues, yet there is no clear consensus even now on what actually happened.

To search for the truth, one should first consider a chronological account of the matter.

The story began on Tuesday, July 1, 1947, when radar installations in New Mexico started tracking an object that zigzagged across the state, exhibiting unconventional speeds and maneuvering ability. On Wednesday, an object was sighted over Roswell. On Thursday, some Washington officials flew in to observe the object.

Late Friday night, the object was lost on radar screens and believed crashed.

Saturday, July 5, Grady L. "Barney" Barnett claimed he, along with some archeologists who happened to be working north of Roswell, discovered wreckage and reported it. The Roswell Volunteer Fire Department was called to the scene, which was on a ranch thirty-five miles north of

Excerpted from chapter 4 of *Alien Agenda*, by Jim Marrs. Copyright ©1997 by Jim Marrs. Reprinted by permission of HarperCollins Publishers, Inc.

Roswell. The rancher, William "Mac" Brazel, found debris scattered over an area three-quarters of a mile long and several hundred feet wide—so much debris that his sheep refused to walk through it. On Sunday, July 6, Brazel drove to town and talked to the sheriff, who suggested that the military be notified. Soon, military units arrived and cordoned off the area. Later in the day, Brazel spoke with air intelligence officer Maj. Jesse A. Marcel and showed him a piece of the debris. Marcel returned to his base and notified higher authorities that something unusual had occurred. By Monday, July 7, a systematic examination of Brazel's field by the military began, including an air search.

Early on Tuesday morning Major Marcel stopped by his home as he returned to the airfield and showed unusual material to his wife and son. The military authorities must have felt the debris did not constitute a serious security problem, for later that morning the information officer of the 509th Bomb Group at Roswell Army Air Field—the only unit armed with atomic weapons at the time—was authorized to issue a press release announcing that the military had recovered a "flying disc." This stirred media interest all over the world. That afternoon, Major Marcel was ordered to fly with the debris to Carswell Air Force Base in Fort Worth, Texas.

Meanwhile in Washington, higher military authorities either learned of new developments—some researchers believe they had learned of the discovery of the main body of the UFO and alien bodies by military searchers—or had second thoughts about publicizing the debris. According to the Associated Press, Deputy Chief of the Army Air Forces Lt. Gen. Hoyt S. Vandenberg moved to take control of the news out of Roswell. On Tuesday evening, 8th Air Force commander Brig. Gen. Roger Ramey from his Carswell office told newsmen that Marcel and others had been mistaken and that the "flying disc" actually was nothing more than a weather balloon. Ramey's weather officer, Warrant Officer Irving Newton, was brought in and identified the debris he saw as belonging to a weather balloon. Photographers were allowed to take pictures of the "balloon" wreckage. Years later, researchers Kevin D. Randle and Donald R. Schmitt claimed the original debris was replaced by balloon wreckage in Ramey's office minutes before newsmen were ushered inside.

Following announcement of the balloon explanation, media interest quickly faded. In those security-conscious days following World War II, with fear of Russian attack becoming a way of life, no one thought to question the official version. There the matter rested until 1978, when Jesse Marcel broke his silence, telling UFO researchers Stanton Friedman and Leonard Stringfield that the object he recovered was not from the earth. Since then, the story of the Roswell crash has become a focal point of UFO research, spawning dozens of books, TV documentaries, and videos.

Conflicting views

There can be no doubt that something dropped out of the skies near Roswell on July 4, 1947. The question is what. Once again, we encounter conflicting mind-sets. One mind-set accepts the official explanation that a secret military balloon crashed, somehow was mistaken for a spaceship by otherwise competent intelligence officers, and was hidden away for security's sake for almost a half-century. Another accepts that a downed spacecraft containing alien bodies was recovered by the military and hidden from the public.

Everyone agrees that no spaceship wreckage or alien bodies have been made public. Therefore, the truth seeker is left with only human testimony and official pronouncements. The basis for accepting the balloon version rests exclusively on government reports, which deny any unusual aspect to the Roswell case. A lengthy recitation of past official lies, disinformation, and deceit should not be necessary to establish that such pronouncements cannot be accepted at face value.

Some recent theories contend that the wreckage actually was a secret test of a ten-balloon cluster device under Project Mogul, which was launched July 3 from Alamogordo, New Mexico, or a secret navy "Skyhook" balloon. If it were either of these devices, competent intelligent officers should have been able to distinguish it from a flying saucer. Furthermore, if this theory is correct, a common weather balloon must have been substituted for the Mogul or Skyhook balloon for the news photographers in Fort Worth, substantiating claims that the air force deliberately deceived the news media and the public. And if they lied about one thing, it stands to reason they would lie about another.

According to several reports, both the debris and alien bodies were taken to Roswell's military hospital, then flown first to Andrews Air Force Base in Washington and on to Wright Field at Dayton, Ohio.

Debunker Curtis Peebles scarcely mentioned alien bodies in his book [*Watch the Skies!*], concentrating instead on the debris as exhibited in Fort Worth. Peebles gave the accounts of only four witnesses, one of whom was Barney Barnett, whose story he correctly discounts, as Barnett's location of the crash site differed from most versions and since investigators in 1990 found that Barnett's 1947 diary contained no mention of the Roswell crash. Peebles was able to state that Barnett's story was "unsupported by any documentation or additional witnesses." After alluding to some of the more outrageous theories concerning the Roswell incident, Peebles smugly concluded, "If all these extraneous stories are removed, one is left only with a few fragments in a field."

Roswell witnesses

On the other hand, consider these "additional witnesses" drawn from the well-documented book *The Truth About the UFO Crash at Roswell* by researchers Randle and Schmitt:

William Woody, watching the skies south of Roswell on July 4 with his father, saw a brilliantly glowing object with red streaks. Unlike other meteors he had seen, it was brighter, the wrong color, and took a long time to fall.

Mother Superior Mary Bernadette, from the roof of Roswell's St. Mary's Hospital, saw a bright light go to earth north of town and recorded the time as between 11:00 and 11:30 P.M. July 4, in a logbook.

Sister Capistrano, a Franciscan nun standing beside Mother Superior Bernadette at St. Mary's Hospital, also saw the object come down.

Cpl. E.L. Pyles, stationed south of Roswell Army Air Field, saw what he first thought was a large shooting star with an orange glow fall through the sky sometime between 11:00 P.M. and midnight.

James Ragsdale, a camper who saw a fiery object crash near his camp on the night of July 4. The next day, Ragsdale discovered a crashed circular craft and small bodies. He fled when the military arrived, thinking he might get in trouble.

Trudy Truelove (a pseudonym), a camping companion with Ragsdale, confirmed his account, stating she also saw the craft and bodies.

Jason Ridgway (a pseudonym to protect the man's identity) saw the crashed object, identified it as a saucer craft, but refused to talk about it for many years. He was a friend of Mac Brazel, the rancher who owned the property.

C. Curry Holden, one of several field archeologists who stumbled upon the crash site, described a "fat fuselage" without wings. He also said he saw three bodies, two outside the craft, one partially visible inside.

No UFO story has captured the imagination of the public as has the reported crash at Roswell, New Mexico.

Dr. C. Bertrand Schultz, a paleontologist working in the area, heard of the crash and bodies from Holden and encountered the military cordon thrown up around the site.

Maj. Jesse Marcel, the Roswell intelligence officer who was first on the scene and announced the crash of a "flying disc," took pieces of strange metal that would straighten out after bending, home to show his family. Although Marcel did not contradict the balloon explanation at the time, in later years he said he was correct the first time about a craft from space and that he was muzzled by military authorities. "It was not anything from this Earth. That, I'm quite sure of," Marcel said. "Being in intelligence, I was familiar with all materials used in aircraft and in air travel. This was nothing like this. It could not have been."

Dr. Jesse Marcel Jr., Major Marcel's son and an Air National Guard flight surgeon, who clearly remembered markings on the metal brought home by his father as consisting of "different geometric shapes, leaves and circles" akin to hieroglyphics. His father told him the metal came from a flying saucer, then had to explain what a flying saucer was to young Marcel.

Col. William Blanchard, Roswell Army Air Field commander, visited the crash site and initially indicated to Marcel that the crash involved something highly unusual, perhaps a Soviet secret weapon. He immediately passed the entire matter up to his superiors. Nothing was said about a balloon.

Maj. Edwin Easley, Blanchard's provost marshal in charge of the military police who guarded the crash site, told researchers a large volume of crash debris was loaded onto trucks and taken to the Roswell base, where it was placed on an airplane. In recent years, Easley said he promised the president he would not reveal what he saw, but indicated he believed it was an extraterrestrial craft.

Sgt. Thomas C. Gonzales, one of the guards at the site, later confirmed the recovery of "little men" with large heads and eyes.

Steve MacKenzie, stationed at Roswell, tracked the object on radar for almost twenty-four hours and then visited the crash site, where he said a major from Washington took charge of the dead bodies, described as small with large heads and eyes. MacKenzie said if the object he tracked had been a weather balloon, secret or not, his superiors would have ordered him to ignore it.

Lt. Col. Albert L. Duran, a member of MacKenzie's unit, has acknowledged seeing the small bodies.

Warrant Officer Robert Thomas flew to Roswell from Washington with a team of experts, including two photographers, early on July 4 after learning of the erratic path of the object. All were on hand at the crash site, according to MacKenzie.

Master Sgt. Bill Rickett, a counterintelligence corps agent, arrived late at the crash site but described what he saw as a curved craft with a batlike trailing edge that had struck front first into the side of a cliff, scattering a great deal of debris. Rickett was assigned to assist University of New Mexico scientist Dr. Lincoln La Paz. According to Rickett, La Paz, apparently unaware of the bodies, concluded the craft was an unmanned probe from another planet.

Sgt. Melvin E. Brown later told family members he helped transport alien bodies from the crash site to a Roswell hanger. He described them as smaller than humans with leathery skin like that of a reptile.

Frank Kaufmann of the 509th Bomb Group staff told of a single large crate that was placed in a cleared-out hanger at Roswell and protected by armed guards. He said he understood the crate contained bodies recovered at the crash site.

W.O. "Pappy" Henderson, a pilot with the 1st Air Transport Unit, flew the crate and debris in a C-54 transport plane to Andrews Air Field in Washington, then on to Wright Air Field in Ohio, according to Steve MacKenzie. Henderson's widow, Sappho, said he had described the debris as "weird" and nothing he had ever seen before. She added that, following a TV special in 1988, Henderson confirmed the descriptions of small recovered bodies.

The story of the Roswell crash has become a focal point of UFO research.

Sarah Holcomb, who worked at Wright Field at the time, told researchers she heard from a crew member that a plane had landed with bodies from a flying saucer. Later the base commander came around and said there was no truth to the story but added that anyone mentioning the "rumor" would be subject to twenty years in jail and a $20,000 fine.

Helen Wachter also was at Wright Field and said she overheard the husband of a friend tell excitedly about the arrival of "alien bodies." At first, she thought he meant people from outside the country, but she quickly understood he was referring to extraterrestrials.

John Kromschroeder, a close friend of pilot Henderson with an interest in metallurgy, said he was given a piece of metal by Henderson, who said it was part of the interior of the crashed craft. Kromschroeder said the metal was gray and resembled aluminum but he was unable to cut it, even using a variety of tools.

Maj. Ellis Boldra, who may have studied the same piece of metal as Kromschroeder, told his family that the fragment was incredibly strong and did not melt when he subjected it to an acetylene torch but in some way dissipated heat.

Floyd and Loretta Proctor, nearest neighbors of rancher Mac Brazel, recalled that Brazel showed them pieces of the debris, which could not be cut or burned.

William Proctor, the Proctors' son, saw a large amount of debris and took some home. Later, according to family members, he was forced to turn it all in to the military.

Sgt. Thomas C. Gonzales, one of the guards at the site, later confirmed the recovery of "little men" with large heads and eyes.

William W. "Mac" Brazel, owner of the crash site, said he heard an explosion during a thunderstorm on the night of July 4 and the next day, along with William Proctor, found a field full of scattered debris and described many big pieces of dull gray metal that was unusually lightweight and could not be cut or burned. Four days later, after being held by military authorities and accompanied by military officers, Brazel told the Associated Press the debris was actually found on June 14 and consisted of string, paper, some tape, and bits of metal that covered no more than two hundred yards in diameter. Oddly enough, he ended this obvious description of some sort of kite or balloon by saying, "I am sure what I found was not any weather observation balloon."

Bill Brazel, Mac's son, said his father was held for eight days by the military and released only after swearing not to discuss the incident. He told his son he was better off not knowing about it but swore what he saw was not a balloon. Bill Brazel said his father was muzzled by military authorities. He also said he handled some of the debris found later on his father's ranch and that it resembled aluminum foil but when wadded into a ball, it would straighten itself out smooth. He too said it could not be cut or burned. The younger Brazel said he showed pieces of the metal to friends.

Sallye Tadolini, the daughter of another of Mac Brazel's neighbors, told researchers that she recalled Bill Brazel showing her a piece of dull-colored metal that he balled up into his fist and, when he opened his hand, returned to its original shape.

Frank Joyce, in 1947 a radio announcer for Roswell station KGFL, confirmed to researchers that Mac Brazel's story after being taken into military custody was "significantly" different from an initial interview. Joyce said that when he talked to Brazel privately, the rancher admitted that he had changed his story but said "he had been told to come in or else."

Glenn Dennis, then a mortician working for Ballard's Funeral Home in Roswell, said about 1:30 P.M. July 5, he received a call from the Roswell base mortuary officer asking if the funeral home could provide a number of small caskets that could be hermetically sealed. Dennis said he realized something strange had occurred when the officer called back and asked how to prepare a body that had been burned or left out in the elements for a time. Later that day, Dennis drove to Roswell Field to deliver an injured airman. At the base hospital he saw strange pieces of wreckage in the rear of an ambulance but soon was chased off by an officer, who told him not to talk or "somebody will be picking your bones out of the sand." A few days later, Dennis said a nurse friend told him she was called in to assist in the autopsy of three "foreign bodies" that gave off an overpowering odor. She said the bodies were small with large heads and hands with four fingers ending in pads that looked like suction cups.

E.M. Hall, former Roswell police chief, confirmed to researchers that he heard Dennis talking about the base requesting coffins for "the bodies from a flying saucer" within days of the incident.

George Bush, whose sister Mary worked as secretary to the base hospital administrator, told researchers he would never forget the day in July 1947 that she came home and told him she had seen a creature from another world.

Chaves County Sheriff George A. Wilcox kept a carton of crash debris left by Mac Brazel but was ordered to turn it over to the military. For some time, Wilcox complained how the military usurped his authority, even barring his deputies from the crash site. Worse yet, Wilcox and his wife, Inez, were told by military police that if he ever talked about the incident, his entire family would be killed.

Barbara Dugger, the granddaughter of George and Inez, said her grandmother quoted military police as saying if anything was ever said about the incident in any way, "not only would we be killed, but they would get the rest of the family." Years later, Inez Wilcox also confided to her granddaughter that a flying saucer had crashed near Roswell.

Frankie Rowe was the teenaged daughter of Dan Dwyer, a Roswell fireman who went to the scene on Saturday morning and later told his family he saw the wreckage of a flying craft, two small dead bodies, and "a very small being about the size of a 10-year-old child." According to Rowe, military authorities threatened her family, and one man told her if she talked about the incident, she would disappear into the desert and never be seen again.

It would appear that the most straightforward explanation of the Roswell story is that a very unusual craft crashed and the occupants . . . were taken into custody by the U.S. military.

Brig. Gen. Arthur E. Exon was a World War II combat pilot who spent time in a German POW camp and later was stationed with the Air Material Command at Wright-Patterson Air Force Base, as it was known after Wright Field and Patterson Field merged. In recent years, Exon became the highest ranking officer to confirm that a quantity of material from Roswell arrived at Wright Field for testing by a "special project" team of lab workers. He said the material was "unusual," looked like foil, but couldn't be dented even by hammers. He also said that he flew over the crash site and was able to see where the craft had come down. Exon added that bodies were found with the main portion of the craft, which ended up in a separate location from the debris.

Naturally, considering the clash of mind-sets, questions have been raised about both the competency and veracity of the Roswell witnesses. But even if half of these witnesses are discounted, the remainder should be more than enough to convince anyone with an open mind that something quite extraordinary occurred at Roswell in the summer of 1947. That the incident stayed on the minds of men in power is illustrated by a story related by William Pitts. A former military man who today is a lecturer for the Society of Manufacturing Engineers, Pitts is the head of Project Blue Book, a private organization sanctioned by the U.S. Air Force to investigate UFO sightings. He said that in early 1977 he and others, including J. Allen Hynek, were summoned to a meeting regarding UFOs by Dr. Frank Press, science adviser to newly elected President Jimmy Carter. "The first question," recalled Pitts, "was regarding Roswell. What did we know about Roswell? I turned it around and asked them what they knew about Roswell and they did not reply. They went on to something else." It was not until more than a year later that UFO researchers began to hear the saucer crash story from Jesse Marcel and interest in the Roswell case was revived.

Different theories

Various theories have been advanced to explain what was recovered at Roswell. These include a Rawin Target weather balloon, a Japanese Fugo balloon bomb, or a V-2 nose cone containing monkeys. None of these theories can explain away all the evidence now available about this event, and if any of these theories are correct, it would still mean the air force deceived the public when the weather balloon story was announced.

Responding to a request by New Mexico Republican representative Steven Schiff, the U.S. General Accounting Office (GAO) conducted a document search on records pertaining to the Roswell incident, which only added to the mystery. In July 1995 the GAO reported, "RAAF (Roswell Army Air Field) administrative records (from March, 1945, through December, 1949) and RAAF outgoing messages (from October, 1946, through December, 1949) were destroyed." Schiff's press liaison, Barry Bitzer, stated, "Having spent 24 years in the military, [Schiff] did express some surprise that those records were destroyed, supposedly against regulations and without traceable authorization." Only two records were found, a unit history report stating that a "flying disc" turned out to be a radar tracking balloon and an FBI teletype stating that the military reported that a high-altitude weather balloon was recovered near Roswell. Of course, it was these two reports—official pronouncements produced only after the official version was conceived—which were used by debunkers to dismiss the Roswell crash story. The FBI teletype was especially odd, as it indicated the Bureau may have been monitoring Roswell base telephones and it clearly stated a "disc" was sent to Wright Field. The teletype read, "[name blanked out] further advised that the object found resembles a high-altitude weather balloon with a radar reflector, but that telephonic conversations between their office and Wright Field had not borne out this belief. Disc and balloon being transported to Wright Field by special plane for examination."

Adding to the confusion were claims that other disc-shaped craft may have been recovered at other times and in other locations. Saucers reportedly were recovered in Paradise Valley north of Phoenix, Arizona, in October 1947; near Aztec, New Mexico, in March 1948; and in Mexico near Laredo, Texas, later in 1948. Any one of the crash stories could have been real with the others acting as red herrings, or all the stories could be false. Information on these crashes is meager compared to Roswell and involved the familiar charges and countercharges of lies and hoaxes.

Even a purported autopsy film of an alien body recovered in 1947 has been offered as proof of the crash recovery. During 1995, Ray Santilli, owner of a small London video distribution company, caused a worldwide clamor by revealing what he claimed was authentic 1947 black-and-white movie film of the autopsy of an alien creature found in New Mexico. At first glance, the film—an "Alien Autopsy" complete with 1940s telephone, clock, and medical instruments and a "real" handheld shaky quality—seemed to offer objective evidence that alien bodies had indeed been recovered in New Mexico.

But the clash between mind-sets quickly engulfed this piece of evidence, along with other problems such as conflicting statements and foot-dragging by the film's owners. Debunkers swiftly went to work attacking the film, and scientists took a standoffish attitude. Dr. Chris Stringer of the Natural History Museum in London said he believed the body was a fake because "It's most improbable that aliens could have evolved to look so like humans."

Arguments raged back and forth about the legitimacy of the autopsy film until even many ufologists grew tired of the issue and it faded into the background—although no one was ever able to prove beyond question that it was a fake. Such is the fate of issues mired in the uncompromising battle between mind-sets.

The most likely explanation

Without resorting to convoluted speculation with little or no supporting evidence, it would appear that the most straightforward explanation of the Roswell story is that a very unusual craft crashed and the occupants—whether dead or alive—were taken into custody by the U.S. military, which then conducted a cover-up.

The military is the key here.

Certainly by the time of the "foo-fighters" [mysterious balls of fire witnessed by World War II pilots], ranking members of the military establishment must have known that something new and unusual was in the skies. Some researchers even contend that authorities became aware of UFOs prior to World War II. Contingency plans must have been drawn up with an eye toward the eventual capture or recovery of unusual aircraft. Such plans would have been activated after an examination of whatever was recovered at Roswell.

It is fact that this period marked a definite turn in the military's response to UFOs. Prior to Roswell, the military had been intensely interested in UFOs and open to the idea that they represented extraterrestrial visitation. But with the knowledge gained from the Roswell incident, the military became secretive and publicly offered every mundane explanation possible to account for UFO sightings. It may even be that the Maury Island affair [a UFO sighting in Puget Sound believed by many UFO researchers to be a hoax] was a military intelligence contingency plan to plant a discrediting UFO story in the public mind that was activated after the Roswell crash. Although the incident reportedly happened on June 21, 1947, there was only the word of [Harold A.] Dahl and [Fred Lee] Crisman to substantiate that date, as it was not reported until after the time of the Roswell crash. And the intelligence background of Crisman added considerable weight to this consideration.

Whether Roswell played any role in subsequent events or not, it is a fact that on September 15—less than four months after [pilot Kenneth] Arnold saw discs soaring over Mount Rainier and only two months after the Roswell incident—President Harry S. Truman signed into law the National Security Act of 1947, which among other things created the National Security Council (NSC) and the air force as a separate branch of service, united the military branches under a Department of Defense, and created America's first peacetime civilian intelligence organization, the Central Intelligence Agency. According to unauthenticated documents—collectively known as the MJ-12 papers—a small, select group of prominent military officers and scientists answerable only to the president was created at this time to deal with UFOs.

4

The U.S. Government Has Suppressed Information About UFOs

Robert Dean, interviewed by Bruce R. Anderson

Robert Dean, a retired U.S. Army sergeant major, is a longtime UFO researcher. He was featured in a video about UFOs titled The Greatest Story Never Told. *Bruce R. Anderson writes for the newsletter* UFO Update AZ.

In 1964, when Robert Dean was stationed at Supreme Headquarters Allied Powers Europe (SHAPE) as an intelligence analyst, he came across a secret document. This report, of which only fifteen copies were made, revealed that American and European military authorities were aware of an extraterrestrial presence on Earth. Further research by Dean revealed that the U.S. government knows of ongoing human contact with alien multidimensional beings. Such knowledge has been kept from most U.S. government and military officials and from the American public.

*B**ruce R. Anderson: When did you first get interested in UFOs?*
Robert Dean: We're going back a few years here. I really became curious in the 50's, even in the late 40's. I was a student at Indiana University when all of this began. The big flaps began around at 1947. Kenneth Arnold [a pilot whose June 1947 sighting of mysterious objects received widespread attention], the rumors, and the fly-overs. I was curious, but I was skeptical. It was a passing interest, I would say.

I really didn't get deeply involved in this thing until 1963 when I was assigned to SHAPE [Supreme Headquarters Allied Powers Europe] in Paris, France. I was a professional soldier most of my adult life, and most of those years were in special operations, special assignments here and there. I led combat troops in Korea 1951. I led intelligence operations patrols in South Vietnam 1970. I've had a long history of interesting, special, unusual assignments, and as a result of my training and background, I had been given a TOP SECRET classification many, many years ago.

But when I was assigned to SHAPE in Paris in 1963, I was given an up-

Reprinted from Bruce R. Anderson, "Interview with Robert Dean," *UFO Update AZ*, Winter 1995–1996, by permission of the publisher.

grade from a TOP SECRET to COSMIC TOP SECRET, and I had to have that to work in the operations division in a place we call SHOC, the Supreme Headquarters Operations Center, which is the NATO war room. COSMIC TOP SECRET is a legitimate classification. It's the highest NATO has. In the United States we have classifications that are at least 40 levels above TOP SECRET. The whole field is so compartmentalized. There are people who have TOP SECRET clearances that do not have access to certain kinds of information. The thing is broken down according to the subject, and your need to know.

In military operations in every service, this security thing has become a nightmare over the years. We created it ourselves. We did it during World War II and during the Cold War years. You can have the highest level of classification in one particular area, and that will not allow you access to information in another area. It's the compartmentalization aspect of it. For example, there are four-star generals who do not know a thing about the UFO phenomena. First of all, they have never been told. Secondly, they have not had access to the information, because under the security system it may have been determined that they didn't have a need to know.

> *There are four-star generals who do not know a thing about the UFO phenomenon.*

I could talk to you about the security problems in this country for hours, because it is one of my biggest complaints. We created a nightmare for ourselves during the Cold War years. We let it get out of hand. Bobby Ray Inman, as a matter of fact, who is a retired admiral, has said repeatedly—he used to be the director of the Central Intelligence Agency, he was the deputy director of the National Security Agency, a four-star admiral, one of our top security people—he said that upon retirement we've got a bunch of people over there that are running loose, out of control. He was referring to Langley and Fort Meade, these two locations where CIA and NSA are located. So there are people who know that we've got ourselves a real problem.

I have a tendency to ramble a bit, so you'll have to get me back on the subject. The reason I am wandering on this subject is that it's a matter of great importance to me, because the security systems that we have created over the years are trashing our constitutional system. The United States Constitution is being trashed by top bureaucrats in the intelligence agencies. Guys in the Department of Defense are totally violating the constitutional process. They're making national policy on this particular issue that we are discussing this afternoon. They do not have oversight. The oversight should be from either the legislative or the executive branches of the government. They are up to their ears in the black budget program, which has reached about $50 billion a year right now, and the black budget systems themselves are a violation of the Constitution. They spend $50 billion dollars of your money every year, of the people's money, and they don't have to go to Congress to account for it or explain where it's going.

A secret NATO document

As a result of your COSMIC TOP SECRET clearance, you came across a document at NATO.

I arrived at SHAPE in 1963, the Supreme Headquarters for Allied Powers in Europe, which is the military arm of NATO, which was located in the little town of Rouquencourt right outside of Paris. My security clearance was upgraded to COSMIC TOP SECRET, so I had access to the war room.

I had heard rumors and gossip. When I arrived in 1963 I had learned of the study that was initiated in 1961. The subject was UFOs. Many of us talked about rumors, gossip, one thing or another, and I was curious, because here we are in one of the top military headquarters in the world, and I learned that they had initiated a study in 1961, because we and the Soviets and the Warsaw Pact people had almost gone to war with each other a few times over the UFO matter. These large, circular metallic objects were flying over Europe, coming out of the Soviet zone over the Warsaw Pact. They would fly in formation at a high altitude, at a high rate of speed, and they would fly obviously under intelligent control, and for awhile the Soviets thought they'd belonged to us, and for a time we thought they belonged to the Soviets. Whenever they would show up over Europe and demonstrated their capability, this high tech that they had, obviously intelligently controlled, the Soviets got all wound up and uptight. They'd go on alert, we'd go on alert, they'd close the Berlin gates and one thing or another. It happened time and time again.

It's important to remember in those years that we are facing each other across a divided Europe, our fingers on the trigger, thumbs poised above the red buttons, and World War III just moments away. The last thing we needed in those years was some kind of unknown, unexpected ingredient being thrown into the pot, and that's what this matter became.

In 1961 an event occurred in early February, in the wee hours of the morning. I believe it was the second of February in 1961 when we almost went to war. It was over in about 25 minutes or so, because they never lasted very long. These things would appear, they'd fly over Europe and get everyone all upset and excited, and they would turn north over the channel and disappear off of NATO's radar over the Norwegian Sea. It was almost a standard pattern.

We and the Soviets . . . had almost gone to war with each other a few times over the UFO matter.

Well, in February of 1961, Air Marshal Sir Thomas Pike was the Deputy Supreme Allied Commander in Europe, the Deputy SACEUR, as we called him. He was a highly decorated British Air Marshal. He was the deputy to my boss, General Lyman Lemnitzer, who was SACEUR. Pike said we've got to do something about this, I learned later, and he said we can't let this continue. We're going to have to find out what the hell is happening. We're getting no help from London or Washington on the subject, which is another story, because in those days there was an enormous French spy ring operating outside of Paris, involving ministers, generals, and admirals. You could read all about it in Leon Uris's excellent book entitled *Topaz*.

Anyhow, we'd get nothing from London or Washington because of the nature of the subject, because anything they would give us would go to Moscow and the KGB in many cases before we got it in SHAPE. This subject, I learned later, was the most highly sensitive subject in all of our modern military history. Nothing was forthcoming from either Washington or London on this subject.

So, Pike initiated an in-house study in 1961 after this event in February to determine what the hell was happening. They called it *An Assessment*, but they gave it a subtitle: *Of a Possible Military Threat to the Allied Forces In Europe*. It was a military study with a military purpose, with no other purpose than to determine if there was a military threat here. It was not a broad-based vast in-depth analysis. It was simply a determination of what was happening, and do we have to be involved. Are we threatened in some way? I think that is important to understand.

In the study, there were [alien] autopsy reports.

The study was three years in its completion from 1961 to 1964. When they published it in 1964, and I was still there working in the war room, they published it in 15 copies, COSMIC TOP SECRET. Copy One went to the Secretary General of NATO, who funded the thing. Copy Two went to General Lemnitzer (my boss), and Copy Three was placed in the vault in the war room. When it was published in 1964—I worked in there sometimes into the wee hours of the morning. When you're bored, sometimes you pull things out of the vault and you read them. And one morning this Air Force controller, a bird colonel, who was in charge of the shift that morning, pulled this thing out of the vault and said, "Here read this, this will wake you up." It not only woke me up, it changed my life. At the time I was a Master Sergeant working in the war room. I was kind of sassy. I thought I was pretty tough. I had a crew cut. I was a no-nonsense soldier. I had some good assignments, and I was in a choice field. I was getting top assignments because of my classification level.

This document, in 1964, shook the shit out of me, and I have never been the same since. It is important that I explain this to you, because this was not a game to me. Prior to reading this document, I had been interested, curious, skeptical, but nothing much more than that. When I saw this thing in 1964, read it, read it repeatedly, studied it, pulled the annexes out, looked at all the annexes, looked at the photographs, the autopsy reports, the detailed analysis of experts all over Europe, it dawned on me that, Jesus, this is not only real, but this is more than real, this is not a joke, this is not science fiction, this isn't fantasy.

Then the implications of it began to hit me, when I began to realize it wasn't simply a matter of hardware and extraterrestrial visitation, because you can get beyond that. That becomes a reality. It's not that difficult to handle. I just kind of assumed that the universe is teeming with intelligent life. But to have it laid in front of you as a reality with the impact of it day after day—the study, the conclusion—it makes an impact that you never get away from.

I am one of those people who do not know how you can walk into this with an open mind, study the evidence that's available, and ever turn your back on it and leave it alone. I don't know how people can do that.

Alien autopsies

You mentioned autopsy reports.

In the study, there were autopsy reports. There had been a crash of a large 30-meter disk in Northern Germany, just about a mile and a half from the Baltic Sea in a little town called Timmensdorfer-strand. It was the early 1960s. This happened in the British zone of occupation. As you know, Germany was divided up among the British, French, and Americans in those years, a carry over from the occupation. When the British Army Engineer Battalion got there, they found twelve small bodies. And when I say small bodies, I'm talking about little dudes, not human. Humanoid, but not human. Three-and-a-half to four feet tall, and sometimes a little more.

But what was so interesting in the autopsy report were the off-the-cuff comments and observations by the medical examiners as they're conducting the autopsy, exclamations like "holy shit," "Jesus Christ," "My god look at this."

The bodies were all the same. There was no reproductive capability that we could determine. There was no alimentary tract, no rectum, no teeth. What were we dealing with here? It's almost like these guys were made in some lab somewhere. They were all identical!

Were there any audio or video recordings of these autopsies?

There were audio recordings. There was no video. We had video back then, but it was not widely used, particularly in the military. The British Engineer Battalion that retrieved the object and the bodies did with what they had. They brought in medical examiners.

I saw photographs of them taking the ship apart. There were photos of them breaking it into wedges. It came apart like a pie. There were roughly about 6 pieces. Then they loaded the pieces on lowboys and hauled them away. I saw photographs, the whole crash, taking the bodies out. There were close ups of the stretchers. There were close ups of the bodies, and they had on some kind of little suits. There were no survivors whatsoever.

There was a fluid in the bodies, but it wasn't like blood. They apparently had lungs and they had a heart, but that was about the only real similarity with a human being. There was no way they ingested or evacuated nourishment, and the question arose, how did these guys get nourished? In the mouth there were four or five little membranes. There must have been some process to ingest the nutrients and to assimilate them, but there was no way to process waste products. These guys had no rectums. There were no sex organs.

Were there any problems dissecting the aliens? Any noxious gases?

Nothing I remember reading about. This was a rather quick kind of a thing. The autopsies were conducted within hours, I would say, of the crash. There have been cases in our country where the bodies have been laying out in the sun or in the desert for few days, and I think that's probably why we have these reports of gas that have been so noxious that upset people so much. I keep hearing that report about Roswell. I think some of these little bodies had been lying in the sun for awhile. I'll tell you first hand that a human body smells pretty bad when it's in the process of decay, but there was no remark that I remember reading that indicated the objects, individuals, whatever they were, had an odor of their own.

The fluid was interesting. They remarked that it was some kind of yellowish, greenish substance, and one of the medical examiners said that, "It reminds me of chlorophyll." There was a heart, a pump that circulated the fluid, and there were apparently a couple of lungs that were just basically to bring in oxygen of some form.

Now bear in mind this is 1964. What was finally put into the SHAPE study, *The Assessment,* were the conclusions reached after stuff that our own military had learned as early as 1949. Operation SIGN, Operation GRUDGE, all of the reports and investigations conducted by the Air Force back in 1940's and 1950's, all had basically reached the same conclusion that the SHAPE Study Investigation had in 1964. But we didn't know that in Europe at the time because the U.S. was not sharing any of this. The only country the U.S. has been open with and shared with over the years was Great Britain.

Two years ago I was visiting in England with the Admiral Peter Hill Norton. Lord Peter Hill Norton was the British Chief of Defense for seven years, equivalent to a five-star admiral. His job was the same as the Chairman of the Joint Chiefs of Staff. He was the number one military man in all of Great Britain. Lord Hill Norton was livid because he had never been given any information during his years as Chief of the British Defense Staff on this subject. His staff, some of them, had lied to him and mislead him. The point I'm getting at is that we and the British did share the information, but apparently they didn't let Lord Hill Norton in on it when he was the chief of the staff.

I believe . . . that the time has come . . . for the American people to be told the truth by their government.

This study, as I told you, was released to all 15 members of the military nations that were involved in the alignment in 1964. Only 15 copies were ever made. When France withdrew from the military alliance in 1967, General De Gaulle threw us out of France. Now, this is another bit of history. I've often thought it tied in with this big scandal involving the spy rings. But in 1967, one of my last duties while I was at the headquarters was to help pack up the headquarters and move it to a new location at Belgium. They built a new multi-million dollar facility outside Brussels, and in the summer 1967 I was in the process of helping move the headquarters. We had an enormous amount of classified material, tons of documents, that had to be moved under controlled situation. *The Assessment* was a part of it. And we were thrown out of France.

Now, De Gaulle remained a member of NATO, but he withdrew from the military alliance, and that is why we had to pack up and leave. When we did so, we required the French to return their copy of *The Assessment*, which they did after about eight weeks of delay, and many of us in the headquarters knew exactly what they were doing. They were copying the damn thing. Not long after that, France established an organization known as GEPAN. It was their own national UFO investigative service. It was a government organization. It was under the Gendarmerie [the French Constabulary].

[pause]

Document still classified

We were talking about The Assessment. *Is there any way the general public can access that document?*

Let me explain a little something. Cecilia [Bob's wife] and I went to Europe two years ago to attend an international conference in Dusseldorf. We took a weekend in between and visited SHAPE. We drove over to Brussels, rented a car, and went on down to Casteau, which is the little town in Belgium near where SHAPE is now located. Because of my background and my ID and my records, I was able to get access to the headquarters. Cecilia and I spent an entire day at SHAPE taking a tour, visiting some of the old departments, trying to find out if any of my old cronies were still around, and sadly enough, no.

I learned, however, from a connection with the Command Sergeant Major that *The Assessment* was still in the files, it was still classified COSMIC TOP SECRET, and it's still considered to be the most sensitive document NATO has.

Now, the Freedom of Information Act is the law allowing United States citizens to have access to material, and it ain't working. Any federal judge in response to a request from NSA or CIA can deny you access. We've gotten releases of documents that were 95% blacked out. [UFO researcher] Stanton Friedman loves to hold them up in front of people and say we got this document from NSA, it's 65 pages, and we've got 3 pages here that we can read. Well, that's my feeling about the Freedom of Information Act, and it doesn't even apply to a NATO document.

We tried to get access to the document itself through some connections with the Admiral Lord Hill Norton. He has a lot of "old boy network" connections. He tried repeatedly to get access to some of the material, and they froze him out! This is a five-star admiral. You know of course you are dealing with the most sensitive issue in the history of the human race. It is the most highly classified sensitive issue in the U.S. military security history. It's a multi-national cover-up.

Has it The Assessment *ever been leaked?*

There have been other old boys like myself who have come forward and said, "Dean is telling the truth, I was there, I saw the thing, I read it." We have a retired Air Force three-star [general] who has said that. There are a couple of admirals who have said that.

I recently heard from friends in Europe that a statement made within the last six months by a retired Soviet Major General KGB confirmed the existence of *The Assessment*. Oleg Kalugan is a retired two-star KGB general. General Kalugan has made a statement to George Knapp or Michael Hesemann saying they knew that NATO had this study. They had a study of their own. He said that we both studied the matter. We both learned quite early on that neither one of us were involved in it and that it was a lot more serious than that.

It kind of pissed me off that it takes a foreign agency like the KGB to confirm the existence of *The Assessment*. That is what's so frustrating about all this. It's the same thing about what happened up in Groom Lake [site of a secret military base]. We had to get a Soviet intelligence agent to testify that Site 51 exists, and we had to use Soviet satellite photography to prove it. There is a recent court case regarding some injuries of guys who were working there.

Bob, you have been researching for 40 years now. Why haven't you written a book?

I have been trying to write a book for at least ten years. I've got a pile of 400 pages of notes, bits and pieces and everything else. The only thing I can tell you is if I could just shut up and stay home I might get it finished. I just got back from a conference in Anaheim where I was invited to speak to the regional MENSA [high-IQ society] convention. I'm leaving Thursday for Kansas City. Then when I get back from there I'll be going to Mexico City, then to Brazil. That's my problem. I'm trying to finish it. I have a title: *The Time Has Come*. I believe that in my heart that the time has come for a lot of things to happen, and the most important is for the American people to be told the truth by their government.

I guess that explains why you have been devoting so much time and effort to this matter.

You know, I began as a curious skeptic and became an interested researcher. I kept digging into classified files up to the day I retired and they pulled my classified security clearance from me. I used to drive some of my friends up a wall. I'd show up, have coffee, get into their files, ask them questions, etc. I have a couple of old cronies that still work at Langley. I have one old friend who is still hanging on at Ft. Meade, which is NSA headquarters, and the "old boys network" still works pretty well. I kept investigating until I retired, and then continued investigating without access to classified documents. I had to do other things. Sometimes I had to buy material, had to violate the law a few times, and I'm not ashamed to admit it.

Mind-boggling implications

Over the years I have become convinced that this subject is not only the most important subject in the history of the human race, but its implications for the species are mind-boggling.

I no longer do the traditional investigations that I use to. I don't go to the sites and pour plaster of paris or look for pieces of metal or whatever. I interviewed people, this and that, but now I stopped. As Alan Hynek has said, we have an over abundance of evidence. We don't need any more.

What we need is two things. One, to put it together and make some sense out of what it means. Two, to get our government, which is supposed to be for, by, and of the people, to tell us the truth, and that's what I am working on now. I'm trying to make sense of what it really means. It's not just the hardware. When I left the military group, we learned that we were dealing with interplanetary visitations. We also knew that we were dealing with interstellar visitations. We were dealing with intergalactic visitations.

Would you be surprised to know that the government does know and is aware that we are having an ongoing involvement with what appears to be multi-dimensional intelligence? Multi-dimensional! Now this blows the physicists out of the water. We are dealing with some intelligent beings that are so far beyond us that we would say they are either gods or it's all magic. We have not come to terms with the fact that there could be civilizations out there that could be a million years ahead of us. Could you imagine what their technology would be like? Multi-dimensional travel, apparently, is commonplace out there. The only people I know of that can really deal with it are quantum physicists and theologians. It's interesting to me that the theologians and physicists are beginning to talk to each other.

Would you be surprised to know that the government . . . is aware that we are having an ongoing involvement with what appears to be multi-dimensional intelligence?

So you would say that the ultimate goal of ufology is to put this information into a package that makes sense.

Yes, Bruce, I believe that people could handle this information. I believe the people are a lot smarter than the government has ever given them credit for. I am a believer in people. I have two focuses of what is left of my life. I'm an old codger now, and I'm getting angry and cantankerous because there is not a whole lot of time left. One is to wake up the American people to this reality and start paying attention and demand some answers, and secondly is to get this whole matter back into the congressional process, the constitutional process, where it should have been in the first place, and get it out of the hands of the military and out of the hands of the intelligence agencies. If we don't do that then the Constitution is finished. That's my primary purpose.

Is there anything that you are currently researching?

Well, I'm currently researching the scandal of NASA. The "old boys network" goes beyond the U.S. military services. I have connections all over the world. Japan, all over Europe, Italy, all over the United Kingdom. NASA was created under a mandate and a statute, which they have repeatedly violated over the last few years. I refer you to *The McDaniel Report* [a critique of NASA calling for research into artificial structures on Mars].

A young Japanese researcher came up to me in San Francisco and said, "I've got some photos to show you." I've never seen these in the U.S. before, but they're appearing now in Japanese books, and according to the books these are NASA photographs. He asked if I had ever seen them before and I replied, "Good god no, where did you get that?" He takes me to the library in Japan town in San Francisco, and we went through the books, and there were NASA numbered and labeled photographs never before released in the U.S. Apollo 12, Apollo 15, Apollo 11. And they have the negative numbers, and I've got copies here which I will share with you.

Now, that stuff is not available to the American people. How the Japanese got it I don't know. I'm now trying to get copies of these documents and the negatives themselves. The University of Arizona is suppose to have a complete catalog of the old Apollo pictures. Would you believe that the one photograph we're looking for is missing? I got this out of a Japanese book published in Tokyo. This is NASA photo #AS12 (Apollo 12), negative #50-7346. It was taken on the way to the moon. They saw an object and they didn't know what it was and they photographed it. That happens to be missing from the negative files over at the U. of A. Here is another one. [Author Richard] Hoagland has the same problem. I'm going to have this made into a poster and share it with the American people and tell them it was made with their own tax money. What do you think that object is?

Swamp gas?

Sure, ha-ha. A self-illuminating massive object that has lights on it, circular, that was photographed by Apollo 12 near the moon. Another thing I'm angry about is that there is a fellow by the name of Maurice Chatelain. He is a defense scholar. He was the director of the Apollo communications program for many years. Chatelain was there in Houston and at Kennedy when they were listening to the guys walking on the moon. He heard first hand what Aldrin, Armstrong, and Conrad said, and it's all there, and he is speaking out now. He was the director of Apollo communications, so he heard first hand what they all saw. For example, "My god, Houston, you have got to see this, this is incredible, they are here, they were waiting for us." Stuff like that.

Has he written a book?

Yes. Here is a copy. The title is *Our Cosmic Ancestors*.

5

Aliens Are Abducting Humans

Marcia Jedd

Marcia Jedd is a journalist and researcher whose work has appeared in newspapers and trade journals.

Poll findings indicate that two percent of the U.S. population—five million people—claim to have been abducted by aliens. Researchers have investigated many abduction accounts using hypnosis and other techniques and have concluded that the alien abduction phenomenon is real, although they disagree on what the agenda of the aliens could be. The experiences of Kate that are described in this article are typical. She has memories of alien encounters since childhood, has been taken on extraterrestrial spaceships and subjected to medical experiments, and has experienced mysterious healings and heightened psychic powers.

Kate first remembers the small, gray creatures visiting her when she was four years old. A female being entered her bedroom and told Kate that her mother had just given birth to a girl. When her father came home from the hospital to tell her the news, Kate was already celebrating her sister's arrival.

Throughout her childhood, the gray beings continued to visit Kate. She remembers seeing them peer into the family's Michigan farmhouse at night. She thought their visits were pleasant—but by the time Kate reached her teens, she realized that other children weren't having similar experiences with their "imaginary friends." Other people reacted negatively to her experiences. At age 15, after a fundamentalist minister assailed Kate for describing her abduction experience, Kate buried her memories. "I didn't talk about it for 28 years," she said.

While Kate's story is astounding, it's not unique. Across the United States, extraterrestrial experts are researching the abduction experience—and they have discovered a number of common features.

Kate's story seems typical. Throughout most of her young adult life, Kate felt compelled to run from the beings, reasoning that by moving to

Reprinted from Marcia Jedd, "What Do Aliens Want?" *Fate*, January 1997, by permission of *Fate* magazine. Copyright ©1997 Llewellyn Worldwide, Ltd.

a new city, they couldn't find her. In the 1970s, Kate was a professional singer, based in New York. One day she visited an apartment building in New Jersey to perform children's songs for a cable television show. As she approached the building, she said she felt "weird vibes" come over her, and she sensed that something out of the ordinary had taken place in the immediate vicinity. Later, she learned there had been a documented sighting at the same building, an incident that was chronicled in Budd Hopkins' book *Missing Time*.

Alien healing

Kate said she has mixed emotions about her experiences with the beings. At times, they have protected her, communicated information to her, and even healed her. In July 1987, Kate attended a retreat on an Indian reservation near Reno, Nevada. During the first night of her stay, she awoke at about 1:30 A.M. to go to the bathroom. As she made her way back from an outhouse, she sensed a presence. "They're here again," she thought. "They want me to go with them. But I don't want to go." Despite her resistance, Kate found herself walking to the opposite side of the lake and down the side of a mountain in the dark. "It was like something was drawing me," she said.

She was led to an alien spacecraft. Once on board, she gazed out a large window to see rocks floating, a distinct blue dot, and a bright white dot. Kate believes they were asteroids, the Earth, and the sun. During her tour of the craft, the beings conducted a medical examination. "They looked inside my uterus and saw damage from a birth control device. They told me they were repairing damage and to expect bleeding," she said. Years prior, Kate had suffered a near-fatal infection from the device. The beings also communicated to Kate that upon seeing an owl, she would forget the experience.

Kate recalls seeing an owl while walking back to the camp at about 4:15 A.M., too tired to think about what had happened.

Some 18 months later, Kate experienced uterine bleeding and underwent a D and C procedure—a scraping of the uterus lining to remove tissue for lab analysis. Kate unexpectedly awoke from the strong anesthesia during the procedure, something her doctors had never seen before. In a cold sweat on the surgical table, Kate felt the memories of the Reno abduction flood back in rich detail.

Extraterrestrial experts are researching the abduction experience—and they have discovered a number of common features.

In 1993, tests indicated cancerous cells on Kate's cervix. Within the next two months, Kate changed jobs and health plans. During this time, she dreamed the beings distinctly told her to "redirect the ribosomes." A few weeks following this vivid dream, Kate had an additional test and began scheduling her cancer treatment. But, miraculously, the new test showed no signs of cancer. Kate has since taken up studying ribosomes, a term she wasn't familiar with. Ribosomes help the body manufacture proteins for new cells and cell repair.

Kate said the alien beings have always been with her. "The beings told me they did things to me before I was born. I believe my abductions happened as a result of pre-birth contact," she says. Both of her parents have mentioned their own experiences. Her niece, nearly three, has spoken of a little gray man, and Kate recalls two instances when she and the child were abducted together. Kate feels she has a special duty to protect her niece, but she believes the beings are also a protective force for the child, who enjoys stable mental health, a happy family life, and an IQ well above average.

Abduction researcher David Jacobs, Ph.D., a Temple University historian and author of *Secret Life: Firsthand Accounts of UFO Abductions*, says abductions run in families. "If an abductee marries a non-abductee, all the kids will be abductees," said Jacobs. Roper poll findings suggest that two percent of the U.S. population, or about five million people, have had experiences consistent with a UFO abduction. Jacobs believes this is a conservative estimate. Typically, he said, a person will have abductions throughout a lifetime, often beginning in childhood or infancy.

The UFO connection

UFOs have a tenuous connection with the psychic world and paranormal events. French astrophysicist and UFO researcher Jacques Vallee said UFOs are physical objects that interact with their environment through the emission of light and other electromagnetic radiation, mechanical and thermal effects, and psycho-physiological changes in witnesses near the phenomena. UFOs also can disrupt electromagnetic patterns, which can wreak havoc on electronic equipment.

While documented UFO accounts date back to the turn of the century, actual sightings of UFOs weren't commonly reported until the 1950s. The modern era of UFOs began in 1947, with a well-documented Washington state sighting and reports of a UFO crash near Roswell, New Mexico. Abductions were not widely known until the Betty and Barney Hill case in 1961, and such reports didn't become prevalent until the late 1970s. Some researchers also suggest, however, that abduction phenomena date back to the turn of the twentieth century. Unfortunately, historical accounts before the second half of this century may be unreliable, Jacobs suggested.

Emerging memories

One characteristic of the abduction phenomenon is the inability of some abductees to remember their experience. Many people don't remember major parts of the abduction until well after the event. The memory may surface after it is triggered by similar situations. Others may not recall abductions until they undergo hypnosis or therapy.

For Kate, memories of her abductions emerged slowly, long before she explored specific incidents under hypnosis. Her full conscious recall of the Reno abduction, for example, was sparked by the D and C procedure, an event directly connected to the examination aboard the alien craft. (The aliens had warned her to expect bleeding, which necessitated the D and C.) Abduction memories also surfaced once she realized others had reported such experiences.

On a routine trip to the drugstore in 1987, Kate suddenly found herself with a copy of Whitley Strieber's *Communion*, a book she had refused to look at before. "That was when I started realizing that the strange dream I was having was something more than just a dream," she said. Around this time, Kate heard a radio talk show about close encounters in California, and she reluctantly called the show to describe her experiences.

One characteristic of the abduction phenomenon is the inability of some abductees to remember their experience.

Kate believes her exposure to the beings has heightened her psychic abilities. Some of her many clairvoyant experiences occurred in the 1980s while living in San Francisco. Once Kate dreamed she was looking at a calendar, seeing a specific date and Pan Am flight number, and then she saw a plane crashing upon takeoff. She felt so strongly about the dream that she stopped in the local Pan Am office the next morning to ask about the flight and describe her dream. Aghast, the reservations agent reported the flight was about to depart from Chicago O'Hare, and Kate urged the agent to communicate potential difficulty to Chicago. The plane was quickly grounded and an inspection uncovered a faulty wing bolt.

Kate habitually records her dreams. On April 15, 1989, she scribbled a note in the middle of the night about one of her dreams. It read: "Mid October, strong earthquake, Santa Cruz mountains." A major Bay Area earthquake occurred on October 17, 1989.

Unquestionably, Kate's gradual acceptance of her abductions have strengthened her convictions about her life's purpose. At 50, Kate is now convinced that other beings exist, in realms beyond the human experience.

"We owe it to ourselves to look at what's going on, rather than ridiculing the people it's happened to and being so sure we know everything," Kate said.

What abduction researchers think

Dr. Richard F. Haines, an abduction researcher and semi-retired research scientist, interviews many abductees using hypnosis. He also investigates UFO sightings by airplane pilots.

"From a strictly scientific point of view, there is no evidence," Haines stressed. He equated the study of abductions to cryptography, in which hidden patterns and symbols are deciphered. But science alone isn't up to the task, Haines suggested. He believes a multidisciplinary team of scientists, scholars, theologians, and mystics should study abductions.

Like Haines, Jacobs assumes the abductions are more than psychological events. "I said, 'Okay, let's assume it is happening.' When you do that, suddenly everything opens up and you begin to realize more details of the phenomena and how it works," said Jacobs, who has interviewed dozens of abductees.

Jerome Clark, editor of the *International UFO Reporter,* vice president of the Center for UFO Studies, and former editor of FATE, agrees that there is no conclusive physical evidence of abductions yet, but he said the phenomenon deserves study. Some cases can be explained as merely psychological fantasies, he said, and a few are arguably real interactions with extraterrestrials (ETs), but the majority of cases are "experience anomalies," contends Clark. "Much abduction material comes out of this murky realm of experience, but they are indeed experiences," he said.

Vallee suggests that UFOs are a front: a disguised interaction between humankind and creator, a deeply rooted communiqué that's been going on for centuries. It began as primitive magic, developing into mystical experiences, fairy-faith, and religion. Vallee cites Carl Jung's theory of the "collective unconscious," which may be the origin of all of our symbols and images. Jung thought of flying saucers or UFOs as a profound archetype, underlying both psychic images and physical shapes.

Physical abductions

Some contend that incidents perceived as abductions may simply be out-of-body experiences (OBEs). However, many researchers report that most cases are physical abductions.

Abduction researchers Budd Hopkins and David Jacobs remain convinced that the abductions are physical, and not merely psychological episodes or out-of-body experiences. "People are physically gone in real time," Jacobs said. In some cases, spouses and family members may also be taken, or they may enter an altered state which discourages their own recall of a missing family member.

Both Jerome Clark and Dan Wright, a member of the Mutual UFO Network (MUFON) who spearheads a large abduction research project, suggest that only a small number of abductions are non-physical, out-of-body experiences. Wright said that many abductees report alien beings who physically enter their bedrooms. "The beings have some sort of mental control. The person is dazed, but leaves with them. There may be a beam of light and they're levitated up into the light, through the bottom or side of a ship," he said. OBEs may not occur until the person is on board the craft.

Abductions, like UFO sightings, can also happen in waves.

In other cases, abductees report that the alien beings take them through closed windows or walls, Wright said. Others are compelled to leave the house themselves, or park their car, then walk to a desolate area and enter a waiting UFO by walking up a ramp.

Length of time varies for abductions, ranging from minutes to days. Most reported experiences last from one to three hours. Abductions generally occur at random, but they can follow distinct patterns, such as specific times in a woman's menstrual cycle. Abductions, like UFO sightings, can also happen in waves.

Abductees are certainly encountering many different levels and types of beings. Some beings have the ability to penetrate matter, but others don't. Most communicate through telepathy. Some are tall and humanoid in appearance, while others are short and gray.

What is the alien agenda?

Why would extraterrestrials want to abduct humans? Jacobs believes the focus is reproduction. He says the vast majority of abductees report generally negative experiences. Aliens reportedly probe humans' bodies, collect eggs and sperm, and leave a wide range of scars—both physical and emotional.

"This is a goal-oriented phenomena. They're not here to enjoy the flora and fauna," Jacobs said. "Once a competently investigated person begins to understand what's happened to him or her, they all talk about reproductive experiences. There are no exceptions to that," states Jacobs.

Other experts aren't so quick to relegate the agenda of all aliens to reproduction or cross-breeding. Many researchers, such as Harvard psychiatrist John Mack and researcher Haines, hint of broader spiritual or evolutionary aspects to abductions. "Who's to say we're not dealing with a spiritual dimension, an unseen dimension, operating independently of us and at will entering our four dimensions?" Haines said.

Some ufologists say the U.S. government may be cooperating with aliens and withholding evidence of their involvement. A number of researchers are currently investigating the government angle. Clark said theirs is a distinctly fringe view, not widely embraced by mainstream ufology.

Whatever the ultimate reasons for abductions, researchers say the phenomenon is here to stay.

6

The UFO Phenomenon Requires Responsible Scientific Research

Bernard Haisch

Bernard Haisch is an astrophysicist, scientific editor of the Astrophysical Journal, *and editor of the* Journal of Scientific Exploration.

The investigation of UFOs currently falls outside the realm of mainstream science. This is unfortunate because the mysterious phenomenon of UFO sightings is worthy of serious scientific research. Stumbling blocks for many scientists who would otherwise be interested in UFOs include the lack of consensus, low scientific reputation, and questionable theories found within the field of ufology. To win public support and funding for UFO research, ufologists should follow the example of the astronomical community and develop research programs and agendas of unimpeachable professionalism and scientific rigor.

The *Journal of Scientific Exploration* (*JSE*), which I edit, is a peer-reviewed research journal in which scholarly investigations on phenomena not part of the currently accepted scientific paradigms may be published. UFO's fall in this category, or more to the point, UFO's certainly fall outside the realm of mainstream science. Is there any possibility of changing this situation? The purpose of this essay is to present some ideas along these lines to the community of UFO investigators and supporters.

By way of introduction I am not myself a UFO researcher, but as editor of this unconventional journal I have been exposed to enough data and met enough serious investigators to become supportive of the need to carefully study whatever this phenomenon, or perhaps phenomena, may be. My profession is that of astronomer and by most criteria, apart from editing *JSE*, I am an insider in the scientific mainstream: author of research papers, principal investigator on NASA projects, associate editor of a leading journal in astrophysics.

The field of astronomy is supported by hundreds of millions of dol-

Reprinted from Bernard Haisch, "UFOs and Mainstream Science," *MUFON UFO Journal*, March 1996, by permission.

lars in government research funding every year, billions if one tallies such major missions as the Hubble Space Telescope. For the January 1996 meeting of the American Astronomical Society in San Antonio, the head of NASA, Daniel Goldin, flew down from Washington just to address us astronomers. Is there any chance that even a fraction of such support and respectability could ever come to ufology?

At the moment, no, not a chance. But as I was listening to Mr. Goldin speaking it occurred to me that some of the points he was making might be worth passing on.

NASA's mission

Goldin made it clear that NASA's job is not to support astronomers (although it does that pretty abundantly, a situation I greatly appreciate!). Nor is NASA's job to employ engineers and astronauts to keep the shuttle flying. NASA's job, said Goldin, is to serve the American people. He mentioned a talk he had given in Bozeman and the excitement that the Hubble pictures elicited there among the ordinary men and women of Montana, far removed from NASA centers. People want to know about the universe. And people especially want to know whether there are other worlds capable of sustaining life. The fact that the announcement at the same astronomical society meeting of the discovery of two new planets orbiting the stars 70 Virginis and 47 Ursae Majoris made the front pages of major newspapers underscores this point.

The search for the origins of life and for other planetary systems is now a cornerstone objective for NASA. Goldin discussed visionary plans to image other solar systems using huge space-based interferometers in the new millenium. He challenged us astronomers to find ways to photograph clouds and mountains on earth-like planets in other solar systems, which must be one of the most scientifically ambitious statements ever made by a head of NASA. This, in his view, is what the American people want from NASA; and I have no doubt that he is correct in his assessment.

I pose to you that there is a lesson here for ufology. If various public opinion polls are to be believed there may be more Americans who believe there is something going on having to do with UFO's than not. It even seems probable, though I do not know this to be the case, that there are more people who "believe in" UFO's than have heard about Hubble. If that is the case, Goldin's lesson for NASA would apply here too. If the American people truly want the UFO problem officially investigated, the government will do that by and by. That does not automatically mean NASA of course. Many appearances to the contrary, UFO's may have nothing to do with outer space as astronomers view the universe.

How would one bring about government-sponsored research analogous to that of astronomy or the other sciences? As Goldin urged us to do on behalf of NASA's research: write, call, visit your representatives and senators. Constituencies count. No doubt about it. NASA funds astronomical research because the American people want this; even if most of it is too esoteric for public consumption, the highlights such as Hubble images and first extra-solar planets do make the newspapers and people read with interest about what their tax dollars are paying for.

But there is a second key ingredient that really needs to come first, and all the grassroots lobbying will come to naught until this second point that Goldin made to us astronomers is translated into action in the wilds of ufology. Given a mandate to support such research, who decides what exactly will be done? Goldin reminded us astronomers that it is our responsibility to come up with NASA's marching orders for the start of a new century. The community of astronomers must reach consensus on prioritizing projects, and he made it clear that those of us whose projects may not make the cutoff, owing to fiscal limitations, are still obligated as members of the research community to support those that are selected. Community consensus and support of an agreed-upon plan, even by those who lost in the proposal competitions, is essential. Without that, the money would eventually stop flowing.

A lack of consensus

And there is the roadblock for ufology. There, in my view, is the principal reason civilian government money has never started flowing, or even trickling. The field is as far from consensus as it could be. There are many possible factors in this ranging from sincere and professionally motivated difference of opinion, to lack of understanding of scientific methods, focus on personal aggrandizement rather than objectivity, paranoia, etc. To be fair to the principles of objectivity and comprehensiveness one must also acknowledge the possibility that the disarray of ufology may be partially driven by official or semi-official disinformation, or even, taking the view of the respected researcher Jacques Vallee, by the UFO phenomenon itself.

But even if those darker possibilities were true, it would still be possible to press ahead if a leadership and a position could be agreed upon, at least a tentative one, a provisional one to get started, one that can be re-evaluated after things get going. One has a better chance of arriving at a destination even if one drives the car in the wrong direction and has to turn around, than if no one is ever selected to start the car and pull out of the driveway!

If the American people truly want the UFO problem officially investigated, the government will do that by and by.

Lest I leave the wrong impression, this is not a solicitation for anyone's vote for this astronomer to lead the charge. I have no desire to become a ufology leader, nor am I here to recommend to you in whom such leadership should be vested. My message is a simple but absolutely realistic one as evidenced by Mr. Goldin's address. Astronomy is doing reasonably well even in today's budget climate because it is meeting a demonstrable desire of the American public and has the professional structure, stature and behaviour to effectively translate that mandate into funded programs.

The public climate is in fact more and more receptive to new ideas and is certainly keenly interested in the possibility of other intelligent life in the universe, including the possibility of evidence for such right here under our noses. It is conceivable that this could be turned into a public mandate for government-sponsored UFO research. But that can only happen if ufologists can somehow follow the successful example of the astronomical community.

This is difficult. Ph.D.'s are not conferred by respected institutions as they are in astrophysics. But there are things that can be done to start the process. Genuinely scholarly papers can be written, which the *Journal of Scientific Exploration* would consider, for example. Note that I am not trying to solicit papers; the *Journal* is highly selective and turns down more articles than are accepted. Journal articles are one way to interest mainstream scientists. In fact, eliciting the interest of mainstream scientists is a key factor in raising the level of UFO respectability. This is extremely difficult in the present environment of disarray, but this could change.

Raising the interests of scientists

A 1977 poll of American astronomers, published in *JSE*, showed the following. Out of 2611 questionnaires 1356 were returned. In response to whether the UFO problem deserved further study the replies were: 23% certainly, 30% probably, 27% possibly, 17% probably not, 3% certainly not. Interestingly, there was a positive correlation between the amount of reading done on the subject and the opinion that further study was in order. Professional researchers would be likely to lose interest if there were complete lack of credible data. This shows a surprisingly high level of potential interest that could be brought into the open if a proper professional structure could be provided. Scientists value their reputations more than anything, and the perceived danger of tainting one's hard won reputation by association with a disreputable activity is a major obstacle.

There is also a kind of non-linear downward spiral. Scientists are both very busy and put off by the appearance of much of ufology. As a result most scientists never look at UFO evidence, which leads to their conclusion that there is no evidence. Given the proper environment this could presumably be turned into a favorable upward non-linearity: Given "evidence of evidence", credibly, soberly presented, the interest of scientists can be piqued, which would presumably lead to the "discovery" by scientists that there is evidence.

Two other obstacles are irrationality and paranoid claims. One cannot avoid the possibility that, as Vallee argues, the element of irrationality may be the actual key and purpose of the phenomenon so as to force a change in human consciousness. This would not be welcome news for the apparently large constituency of nuts-and-bolts saucer enthusiasts, nor presumably for those who take all abduction reports at face value. And this would be very difficult for science to deal with because it is at first glance a frontal assault on science itself. But consider the advent of quantum mechanics and relativity in the early 1900's. These were frontal assaults on the prevailing classical physics that must have looked like madness to many physicists of the day. We do not read about them of course. The textbooks discuss the Einsteins and Plancks and other geniuses who prevailed, not the army of "ordinary physicists" whose careers and worldviews looked to be shattered by what must have seemed irrational to them. But life went on and science even advanced!

Scientists are also certainly not used to the possibility that a phenomenon under investigation may be subject to clandestine manipulation. This may be the greatest obstacle because of the, in my view, small possibility that there may be some truth to it. It is not hard to imagine that there may be a great deal of classified information, but that would not by itself imply any greater comprehension concerning the nature of the phenomenon by those holding—and withholding—the data. The *Journal of Scientific Exploration* is publishing formerly classified information concerning multi-million dollar remote viewing (ESP) programs funded by the CIA and other intelligence agencies over the past 20 years. Projects that were highly secret a decade or two ago are now a matter of public record.

This demonstrates two things directly analogous to the UFO situation: yes, there really were classified ESP programs as claimed; but no, the vaunted government agencies were not able to come to deeper conclusions regarding the nature of that phenomenon than was then or is now publicly available. (The two public reports—by Jessica Utts and by Ray Hyman—on this 20-year effort disagree on the strength of the evidence for remote viewing. The view of the three leading figures in this program, Harold Puthoff, Russell Targ and Edwin May, with all of whom I have had in-depth discussions, is that there were astonishing successes in a fraction of the cases. Unfortunately there was no way to distinguish in advance what would be signal from what would be noise, hence the program could not achieve its required operational intelligence potential.)

Evidence needs to be properly analyzed and then properly presented using techniques . . . of mainstream science.

Only in the unlikely circumstance that the most paranoid vision of government conspiracy with non-earthly intelligences should prove to be true would the existence of classified programs obstruct a successful, open, funded research initiative: either by blocking outright the establishment of an open research program, or by turning it into a sham to further cover "the top secret truth." In any case, nothing would be gained by letting suspicions of this sort stop the attempt to establish an open research program. Indeed, such efforts would perhaps point to valuable indicators of opposition, if such there were.

Something is happening

It seems from my unique vantage point as both scientist and editor of *JSE* that substantial evidence exists of "something going on". But in the real world of competition and politics and entrenched positions that by itself will not move the UFO debates off square one. Evidence needs to be properly analyzed and then properly presented using techniques and venues as close as possible to those of mainstream science. The disparity of the evidence appears to be confusing enough without layers of unproven theory and conspiracy. Somehow out of organization of evidence there could arise not the truth—that is too much—but there could arise a consensus on simply what to do next, who would plan it, who would execute it, how would money be spent in a responsible, accountable, way if made available. The outcome would not be "the answer" but merely and sufficiently the input for the next logical follow-on. If such a scientifically-oriented process could be started, scientists could be attracted; grassroots political lobbying could then point to realistic funding opportunities that a representative or senator would be willing to vote for and tout at the next election as his or her contribution to the legitimate needs and wishes of the public.

Even if the UFO phenomenon should turn out to be deeper than we imagine, even should it prove to transcend science as we know it, the scientific approach is the only feasible way in the real, political, economic, technological world we live in to give us some chance to control our dealings with this phenomenon, rather than letting the phenomenon entirely control us . . . if such it is.

Quo vadis [whither are you going], ufology?

7

The Existence of Extraterrestrial Spacecraft Is Unproven

Alan Hale

Alan Hale is an astronomer, author, and co-discoverer of Comet Hale-Bopp.

The extraordinary claim that UFOs are vessels in which alien beings have traveled to Earth from other parts of the universe requires direct and convincing evidence before it can be accepted. Such evidence, including credible contact with aliens, is thus far lacking. Sightings of mysterious lights in the skies do not constitute direct evidence because people are unfamiliar with the many natural and artificial phenomena that can create UFOs. In addition to making observational mistakes, UFO witnesses may also in some cases be victims—or instigators—of hoaxes. While intelligent life may perhaps have evolved at other sites in the universe, the distances between the stars are so vast as to make interstellar travel unlikely.

W hen I am confronted with beliefs about UFOs or other paranormal phenomena—or, for that matter, just about *anything*—I am guided by three basic principles, to wit:

1) Extraordinary claims require extraordinary evidence. The discovery that there are other intelligent beings in the universe—and, as a corollary, that life and intelligence can and has evolved at locations other than Earth—and that, moreover, these beings are visiting Earth on a semi-regular basis in spacecraft that seem to defy the laws of physics as we now know them, would unquestionably rank as the greatest discovery in the history of science, and most definitely is an extraordinary claim. Therefore, in order for me to accept it, you must produce extraordinary evidence. What might this evidence be? For one thing, the aliens themselves. Not some story where someone says that someone says that someone says that they saw aliens, but the actual physical aliens them-

Reprinted from Alan Hale, "An Astronomer's Personal Statement on UFOs," *Skeptical Inquirer*, March/April 1997, by permission of the Center for Inquiry.

selves, where I and other trustworthy and competent scientists and individuals can study and communicate with them. I'd like to examine their spacecraft and learn the physical principles under which it operates. I'd like a ride on that spacecraft. I'd like to see their star charts and see where the aliens come from. I'd like to know the astronomical, physical, chemical, and biological conditions of their home world and solar system, and how they compare with and contrast with ours. If possible, I'd like to visit their home world, and any other worlds that might be within their sphere of influence. In other words, I want the aliens visible front and center, where there can be *no reasonable doubt* as to their existence. Stories about "lights" or "things" in the sky do not impress me, especially when such reports come from people who have no idea of the vast array of natural and man-made phenomena that are visible in the sky if one would only take the time to look.

The simplest explanation—to me, anyway—for the UFO phenomenon is that every report is either a hoax or is a mistake of some sort.

---

2) The burden of proof is on the positive. If you are making an extraordinary claim, the burden is on you to produce the extraordinary evidence to prove that you are correct; the burden is not on me to prove that you are wrong. Furthermore, you must prove your case by providing the direct and compelling evidence for it; you can't prove it by eliminating a few token explanations and then crying, "Well, what else can it be?"

3) Occam's Razor: If one is confronted with a series of phenomena for which there exists more than one viable explanation, one should choose the simplest explanation which fits all the observed facts. It is an undeniable fact that many people have seen, or at least claimed to see, objects in the sky and on the ground for which they have no explanation. But it is also an undeniable fact that people can make mistakes about their observations. It is an undeniable fact that reports can come from people who are unaware of the various phenomena that are visible in the sky and from people who are not equipped or trained at making reliable scientific observations. It is an undeniable fact that a person's preconceived notions and expectations can affect his/her observations. It is an undeniable fact that some people will lie and will create hoaxes for any one of various reasons. Taking all these undeniable facts together, the simplest explanation—to me, anyway—for the UFO phenomenon is that every report is either a hoax or is a mistake of some sort. If this explanation is incorrect, then you have to increase the sphere of undeniable facts; and for this, see points 1) and 2) above.

Direct evidence is lacking

To me, it seems extremely likely that life has started and evolved at other sites throughout the universe, quite possibly in a great number of places. It also seems rather possible that, at some of those sites, evolution has created an intelligent species which has developed technology far in advance of our own and which might be capable of interstellar space flight. Despite the incredible distances between stars, and despite the vast dispersion in evolutionary states that must exist throughout the sphere of races that have achieved some sort of sentience, it is possible—although, to me, extremely unlikely—that one or more of these races has visited Earth within the relatively recent past. Indeed, I would be absolutely ecstatic if any such visits have taken place. No one would be happier than me to meet with and converse with these beings and, I dare say, there are very few people who are better prepared intellectually and emotionally to deal with this prospect if it were to occur. But again, I want the direct evidence for their existence; I want the aliens themselves. I don't want to hear stories about some "thing" that some person somewhere might have seen.

As a lifelong amateur astronomer, as a professional astronomer, as someone who has read countless science fiction stories and scientific essays, I have devoted my life to unraveling the secrets of the universe and to pushing humanity and humanity's knowledge as far into space as I can. (This is my reason for claiming that there are few people in the world who are better prepared than I am to meet with an alien race; if there is any human being who *could* meet with alien beings, it would be someone like me.) At the same time, I suspect there is hardly anyone who watches and studies the sky more than I do, and while I have almost continuously observed the sky for most of my lifetime, I have yet to see a single object for which there was not a prosaic explanation. I *have* seen such diverse phenomena as: fireballs, rocket launches, satellite re-entries, comets, auroras, bright planets, novae, orbiting satellites, ionospheric experiments, high-altitude balloons—all of which have been reported as "UFOs" by uninformed witnesses. If indeed there are alien spacecraft flying around Earth with the frequency with which UFO devotees are claiming, then I must ask how come I have never seen anything remotely resembling such an object, while at the same time I have managed to see all these various other types of phenomena.

While I have almost continuously observed the sky for most of my lifetime, I have yet to see a single object for which there was not a prosaic explanation.

In summary, I consider it likely that there are advanced alien races somewhere "out there," and I remain open to the possibility that, unlikely as it may seem, one or more such races could be visiting Earth. But if so, where are they? If they possess the technology capable of traveling interstellar distances, then they are so far ahead of us that there can be no reason for them to be afraid of us. If they wish to hide from us, they could do so easily; if they don't wish to, then they have no need to play games with us and only show themselves to a few unwitting individuals. Let them reveal themselves to humanity at large, to our scientists, and to me.

8

Most UFOs Can Be Readily Explained as Natural or Manmade Phenomena

Philip J. Klass

Philip J. Klass is a science writer and UFO researcher. His books include UFOs: The Public Deceived *and* The REAL Roswell Crashed Saucer Coverup.

Most UFOs (Unidentified Flying Objects) are really MPOs (Misidentified Prosaic Objects) such as planets, bright stars, meteors, airplanes, and reentering rockets and space debris. The human mind can play tricks on the observer and make these objects appear like flying saucers. Unexplained UFO sightings often require months of investigation before they can be explained. Even if an explanation is never found in some cases, however, that does not mean that one should jump to the conclusion that extraterrestrial vessels exist.

D espite widespread media coverage of UFOs (Unidentified Flying Objects), one important and well-demonstrated fact is seldom mentioned: At least 90 percent of all UFOs are really "Misidentified Prosaic Objects," or MPOs. More than one-third of all UFO reports are generated by bright planets, stars, meteor-fireballs, and even, occasionally, by the moon.

For example, the March 20, 1975, edition of the Yakima, Washington *Herald-Republic* carried a front-page feature stating that three credible local citizens reported seeing a bright UFO in the western sky around 9 p.m. and watched it for about 45 minutes "until it disappeared." One man, who described the UFO as being cone-shaped with a "greenish-bluish light at the top and a sort of pale flame light at the bottom," said he had never seen anything like it before. Not surprisingly, the front-page story prompted other Yakima citizens to look for a UFO that night.

The next day's edition reported that many more persons had called in to report seeing the UFO, which had returned to the western sky that night at about the same time. The following day, the newspaper reported

Reprinted from Philip J. Klass, "A Field Guide to UFOs," *Astronomy*, September 1997, by permission of the publisher.

that its staff had been "swamped by calls by people mystified and convinced they were seeing an alien craft from outer space."

Fortuitously, one of the callers was an amateur astronomer who, after reading the two previous newspaper articles, had decided to take a look at the UFO. He reported it was the then bright planet Venus. Commendably, the *Herald-Republic* reported the UFO's identification on its front page, whereas many newspapers would have buried the explanation at the bottom of page 18.

There is scant scientifically credible data on the relationship between MPOs and UFOs. Since 1969, when the U.S. Air Force formally ended its 20-plus-year investigation of UFO reports and closed down its Project Blue Book office, nearly all of the people who now investigate UFO reports want to believe that some UFOs represent visitations by extraterrestrial spacecraft.

Despite many reports of UFO landings and persons who claim to have been abducted and taken aboard a flying saucer, no one has yet come up with a single credible physical artifact to confirm the ET hypothesis. The "physical evidence" found at alleged UFO landing sites typically consists of broken tree branches, or small holes that could be the work of wild animals, or a hoaxer. Not one of the many so-called "abductees" has come back with an ET souvenir or any new ET scientific information which could be verified to confirm their tale.

Because nearly half a century of UFO investigation has failed to yield a single, scientifically credible physical artifact, the only evidence supporting the ET hypothesis rests entirely on "unexplained" UFO cases. If an investigator is unable to find a prosaic explanation for a UFO report, believers in the ET hypothesis cite this as evidence that the UFO report was generated by an ET craft.

Because nearly all of the persons who now investigate UFO reports are eager to find "unexplainable" cases, this gives them scant incentive to conduct a rigorous investigation of a tough case. During my more than 30 years of investigating UFO reports, several cases required many months of part-time effort to find a prosaic explanation and one required more than two years.

UFO investigators

A notable exception is the UFO investigative work of Allan Hendry, who became the chief investigator for the Center for UFO Studies (CUFOS), shortly after he graduated from the University of Michigan in 1972 with a B.A. in astronomy and illustration. CUFOS had just been created by J. Allen Hynek, who then headed Northwestern University's astronomy department.

In the late 1940s, the Air Force hired Hynek as a consultant after it discovered that bright celestial bodies generated many UFO reports and that even experienced military pilots sometimes chased after a UFO that turned out to be a bright planet or star. At the time, Hynek was teaching astronomy at Ohio State University—not far from the Project Blue Book offices in Dayton. In 1969, when the Air Force decided to close down Project Blue Book, it terminated Hynek's contract. Several years later he created CUFOS and hired Hendry as its full-time UFO investigator.

For Hendry, with a long-standing interest in UFOs, it was an exciting opportunity. Although Hynek had been a hardnosed skeptic about the ET hypothesis when he was first hired by Project Blue Book, in his later years he became more "open-minded." He hoped that CUFOS could conduct a competent scientific investigation into the UFO mystery. To encourage UFO reports by law enforcement officers, who were considered to be more reliable than the general public, CUFOS obtained a toll-free 800 telephone line whose number was given to many police departments.

During the next 15 months, Hendry personally investigated 1,307 UFO reports submitted to CUFOS—many more cases than any other investigator up to that time, or since. The results were published in 1979 by Doubleday/Dolphin in a book entitled *The UFO Handbook: A Guide to Investigating, Evaluating and Reporting UFO Sightings.*

Causes of UFO reports

Hendry's book—regrettably long out of print—provides the most recent scientifically credible data on the many different "trigger mechanisms" which generate UFO reports. Earlier Project Blue Book data is criticized by some who charge that the Air Force's eagerness to explain away UFO reports resulted in unrealistic explanations. Hendry's data is not vulnerable to such charges because he admitted he would like to find evidence that some UFOs were ET craft.

Of the 1,307 UFO cases that Hendry investigated, he found prosaic explanations for 91.4 percent of them, leaving 113, or 8.6 percent, unexplained. However, Hendry conceded that 93 of these 113 unexplained reports had possible prosaic explanations. This left only 20 cases, or 1.5 percent of the total, as seemingly unexplainable in prosaic terms. Is that evidence that some or all of these 20 unexplained cases involved ET spacecraft?

> *Nearly all of the people who now investigate UFO reports want to believe that some UFOs represent visitations by extraterrestrial spacecraft.*

Hendry wisely resisted making any such claim. In the closing pages of his book, he admitted that rigorous investigation alone is not always sufficient to find a prosaic explanation, which sometimes depends on "sheer luck." (Based on my own investigations over the past 30 years, I fully agree.) Another factor, which Hendry does not mention, is that with his other CUFOS duties, which included producing a monthly publication for subscribers, he could spend an average of only two hours in his investigation of each case. Some of the cases I have investigated have required many dozens or hundreds of hours of effort to find a prosaic explanation.

Early in my own career as a UFO investigator, I was "taken in" by several hoaxers who seemed at first to be honest. I suspect that at least several of Hendry's "unexplainable" cases are hoaxes and that he was too trusting, as I had been.

In the concluding pages of Hendry's book, he commented: "How can

I be sure if my remaining 'UFOs' aren't simply Identified Flying Objects [i.e., Misidentified Prosaic Objects] misperceived (sincerely) to the point of fantasy? The emotional climate about the subject (as revealed by Identified Flying Objects) appears to be adequate to support such a hypothesis for a great many UFO situations, if not all. . . . With our current inability to fully draw the distinction between real UFOs and IFOs, fantasies or hoaxes, coupled with a heated emotional atmosphere, I can only assert that it is my feeling that some UFO reports represent truly remarkable events." But Hendry admitted that "while science may be initiated by feelings, it cannot be based on them."

Mistaken identity

Hendry's investigation showed that nearly 28 percent of all UFO sightings reported to CUFOS proved to be bright stars and planets. Hendry noted that UFOs that turned out to be celestial bodies were often reported to "dart up and down," to "execute loops and figure eights." Occasionally the celestial UFO was reported to "meander in square patterns" or "zigzag." In 49 cases triggered by a bright celestial body, the witnesses estimated the UFO's distance at figures ranging from 200 feet to 125 miles.

When I first entered the UFO field, I would have challenged the idea that an intelligent person could mistake a bright celestial body for a UFO that was "following them." But numerous incidents, some involving law enforcement officers, have convinced me otherwise. If a person driving in a car sees a bright celestial object ahead and suspects that it might be a UFO, and accelerates to try to get closer, no matter how fast the driver goes, he/she cannot seem to gain on the UFO. If the driver then stops and gets out of the car, the "UFO" seems to halt also, because it is getting no bigger or smaller. Now, if the driver decides to return home, the "UFO" seems to be following the car because it remains the same size and brightness.

It might seem surprising that 22 of the UFO sightings reported to CUFOS turned out to be triggered by the moon. Early in my career as a UFO investigator, I was challenged to explain an incident that had occurred with a Navy aircraft crew on February 10, 1951, while en route from Iceland to Newfoundland. The Project Blue Book files listed the case as "unexplained." After careful study of the crew's report, many hours of investigation, and a bit of luck, this UFO could be identified as the upper tip of a crescent moon which was barely visible at the horizon.

Hendry's investigation showed that nearly 18 percent of all UFO reports were generated by advertising airplanes, which carry strings of lights that spell out an advertising message. When seen at an oblique angle, their strings of flashing lights are perceived as being saucer-shaped. When the pilot decides to turn off the lamps and go home, observers report that the "UFO mysteriously disappeared."

UFO incidents

On June 5, 1969, the flight crews of two east-bound airliners flying above 30,000 feet near St. Louis, Missouri, as well as a military jet fighter pilot, reported a near mid-air collision with a "squadron" of hydroplane-shaped UFOs. The incident occurred around 6 p.m., in broad daylight. The military pilot reported that at the last minute the UFOs seemed to maneuver to avoid a collision—which could be interpreted as evidence that these objects were "under intelligent control."

Thanks to Allan Harkrader, an alert newspaper photographer in Peoria, Illinois, who was able to take a photo of the UFOs, they could be easily identified as flaming fragments of a meteor-fireball blazing through the atmosphere on a horizontal trajectory. As a meteor enters at very high speed, it ionizes (electrifies) the surrounding air, creating a long, luminous tail. The two airline flight crews and the military pilot, understandably, assumed that the luminosity was the result of sunlight reflecting off metallic objects.

Based on Harkrader's photo and other reports from ground observers, scientists at the Smithsonian Astrophysical Observatory were able to calculate the approximate trajectory of the fireball. They concluded that the fireball actually passed about 125 miles north of St. Louis, at an altitude many thousands of feet higher than the two airliners and the jet fighter. The same fireball fragments were seen by a private pilot who had just landed in Cedar Rapids, Iowa. He filed a report on the incident with the Federal Aviation Administration's office in which he estimated the objects had flown directly over the airport's east-west runway at an altitude of only 1,000 feet. His distance estimate was in error by roughly 100 miles.

Some of the cases I have investigated have required many dozens or hundreds of hours of effort to find a prosaic explanation.

On March 3, 1968, at approximately 8:45 p.m., a group of three people in Nashville, Tennessee, saw what appeared to be a giant saucer-shaped UFO pass over them in eerie silence at an altitude estimated to be only 1,000 feet. In a detailed report later submitted to the Air Force, they reported seeing many rectangular windows, illuminated from inside the craft.

The Air Force also received a report of the same incident from a group of six people in Shoals, Indiana, 200 miles to the north. They described the UFO as being more cigar-shaped, with a rocket-like flame in the rear, but they too reported seeing rectangular windows, illuminated from inside. They reported its altitude was "tree-top level."

This UFO proved to be the flaming reentry of a Soviet rocket that had been used to launch the Zond-4 spacecraft on a simulated lunar mission. As the rocket reentered at high speed, it broke into fragments which were heated to incandescence, which is what the observers in Nashville and Shoals saw. Once they concluded that this was a UFO, then the flaming fragments "became" windows illuminated from inside the craft. And their brains, unwittingly, supplied details of the craft's shape—based on what the observers had earlier read or heard about the shape of UFOs.

One of the universal characteristics of UFO reports generated by fireballs or reentering space debris is that the object always seems to be much closer than it actually is. In Hendry's book, he reported that nearly 9 percent of the 1,307 UFOs reported to CUFOS proved to be fireballs or reentering space debris.

Hendry, who retired from "UFOlogy" shortly after his book's publication and has never returned, discovered there are many, many trigger mechanisms for UFO reports besides bright planets, fireballs, reentering space debris, and the moon. These included hoax hot air balloons, weather and scientific balloons, missile launches, birds, and kites, to cite but a few.

A UFO or a kite?

Several years ago, shortly before I was to give a UFO lecture to the Seattle chapter of the Institute of Electrical and Electronics Engineers, I was standing outside the lecture hall chatting with several attendees. Suddenly, one of them pointed skyward and said, "What's that?" I looked up and there was a small, orange object which seemed to be hovering at an altitude of several thousand feet.

Someone said: "It looks like a kite." I responded: "No, it's much too high to be a kite, maybe it's a weather balloon reflecting the nearly setting sun." The other party responded: "It can't be a balloon, it's not moving." Suddenly, a third man spoke up: "I think I have some binoculars in my car," and he hurried to get them. He returned with the binoculars, took a brief look and said: "It's a kite." When I viewed the UFO through the binoculars, I agreed.

Were it not for the happenstance that this man had a set of binoculars, I would have to admit that I saw a "UFO" in Seattle that appeared to be too high to be a kite and too stationary to be a weather balloon. But it was not doing anything extraordinary—or extraterrestrial.

There are many, many trigger mechanisms for UFO reports.

For 45 years I have been writing for *Aviation Week & Space Technology* magazine—for 34 years as one of its senior editors and since my "active-retirement" in 1986, as a contributing editor. The magazine has published more articles on space travel than any other publication in the world. I can think of no more exciting story it could publish, or that I could write, than to be able to report that I have finally found a UFO case that defies any possible prosaic explanation. I would expect to win a Pulitzer Prize, a giant bonus, and great fame. So far, I've had no luck. But who knows, perhaps tomorrow—or next week.

9

Extraterrestrial Spacecraft Did Not Crash in Roswell, New Mexico, in 1947

Keay Davidson

Keay Davidson is a science reporter for the San Francisco Examiner *and the author of* Wrinkles in Time *(with George Smoot) and* Twister.

The famous extraterrestrial spacecraft that crashed in Roswell, New Mexico, and the alien corpses recovered and hidden by the U.S. government are fables with no basis in fact. The theories spawned by the Roswell incident constitute an apt example of the mass hysteria movements that periodically occur in American history. The entertainment industry has capitalized on the Roswell myth, marking it indelibly on the American consciousness. Recent research has shown that the wreckage that was recovered in Roswell in 1947 was from a secret military project (Project Mogul) in which a large military balloon was launched to detect Soviet atomic bomb tests. However, no explanation, argument, or proof will convince those who staunchly believe in UFOs.

L ight up the birthday cake: The "flying saucer" movement is 50 years old this month [June 1997]. But it's a bleak anniversary for America's No. 1 pseudo-science. After a half-century of mostly harmless shenanigans—faked UFO photos, alien "encounters" and the like—this sideshow of trash culture has suddenly spilled blood.

On March 26, 1997, news tickers hummed with the shocking, Jonestown-like tale from San Diego County: 39 UFO cultists had donned Nikes, swallowed drugs, secured plastic bags around their heads, and expired. The devotees of Heaven's Gate expected their souls to fly to a UFO accompanying Comet Hale-Bopp on its latest pass by the Sun.

It seems fitting that the 39 dead died in the American West, a traditional testing ground for new myths and delusions. Throughout American history, settlers have gasped at the West's natural grandeur and cloudless horizons and concluded: Anything is possible. Out here, on the

Reprinted from Keay Davidson, "How the West Was One—a Journey into Time, Space, and Pseudo-science," *San Francisco Examiner Magazine*, June 1, 1997, by permission.

wave-battered coast and the wind-swept plateau, hope springs eternal; misunderstood geniuses come to spread their wings, as do screw-ups in search of a second chance. Hence Western genealogies are full of snake-oil salesmen, rainmakers, land speculators, pyramid schemers, gurus and faith healers.

And now, UFOlogists.

Since 1947, flying saucers have been reported around the world, but the UFO movement's roots are as Western as palm trees and Monument Valley. The first "wave" of saucer sightings began in the West in 1947. The wildest UFO cults, like the suicidal Heaven's Gate, have always gravitated here.

And the Homers of the saucer age are the screenwriters of Hollywood. Via film spectacles such as *Independence Day* and TV megahits like *The X-Files*, they transmit UFO lore to the outside world. Thus they keep alive the grandest—and, as we shall see, phoniest—of UFO fables.

The fable is so famous that it is widely known by one word: Roswell. On *Seinfeld*, when the dotty Kramer gasps, "Roswell!" the audience laughs in recognition. For those of you who spent the last decade in a cave, here is the Roswell legend, short version:

In mid-1947, a stricken UFO fell from the sky and crashed on the arid plain near Roswell, N.M. U.S. troops sealed off the crash site. Dead aliens were found inside the wreckage. The corpses were hauled to a secret government laboratory, where they now float within giant vats. Since then, for reasons known only to the CIA, the Defense Department and the White House, the U.S. government has denied the reality of alien visitors.

Meanwhile (the story goes) the extraterrestrials continue to arrive. By night these bug-eyed entities, which resemble anorexic Pillsbury Dough Boys, kidnap sleeping Americans and conduct weird experiments on their bodies. Perhaps they hope to merge our genes with theirs and create a new life form, a galactic super-race. They do this (some assert) with the covert support of U.S. government officials, many of whom are themselves aliens.

The Homers of the saucer age are the screenwriters of Hollywood.

Paranoid? Of course. But Americans have always been a tad paranoid, as the historian Richard Hofstadter observed while the embers of McCarthyism still glowed. Early Americans knew their young democracy was a uniquely fragile enterprise; naturally they feared for its future. The last three centuries have brought repeated waves of mass hysteria, as Americans flail against invisible, exaggerated or nonexistent threats to freedom—Salem witches, Masons, "Papists," the Rothschilds, Communists, Satanic priests, the Protocols of Zion, the Trilateral Commission, the Illuminati, extra gunmen on the grassy knoll . . . and now, aliens.

In the bizarre world of UFOlogy, a generation gap is yawning. The Heaven's Gaters were mostly middle-aged and elderly folk, a generation of UFO buffs who thought the aliens are our friends. They had grown up on such pro-alien films as *The Day the Earth Stood Still*, in which the aliens wanted to help us—here's a cure for cancer, take it!—and urged us to stop playing around with those awful atomic bombs.

GenXers are more cynical. They've grown up on *Independence Day*, with its genocidal aliens in Manhattan-sized saucers, and *The X-Files*, whose sad-eyed stars weekly witness ghoulish conspiracies behind the cheerful facade of American life. For the '90s generation, Roswell is Dealey Plaza [the site of John F. Kennedy's assassination]—the setting for a mythic betrayal of democracy, 50 summers ago, after which the world would never be the same.

What actually happened at Roswell?

Everyone agrees on the basic facts: In June or July 1947, a puzzling object crashed and shattered in the arid lands around Roswell. Winds blew the debris across the landscape. The debris was noticed by one W.W. "Mac" Brazel, a sheep ranch farmer near Roswell. He hauled the junk to the sheriff's office. The sheriff alerted Roswell Field, a local military base, home of the 509th Bombardment Group. The brass investigated. After some initial confusion (including the issuance of a tongue-in-cheek press release about the recovery of a "saucer"), officials announced their conclusion: The debris was a downed weather balloon, that's all.

Meanwhile, rumors spread that the object really was a saucer; that the "balloon" story was a cover-up; that alien bodies had been found in the wreckage.

About that time, Karl Pflock was a young boy living in San Jose. "In the summer of '48 or '49, I was 5 or 6 and we went to a backyard birthday party for the son of one of my dad's employees," he told me. "I remember sitting on the tailgate of a surplus Army truck and listening to several of the dads talking about those "flying saucers." One of them was telling the story of a crashed flying saucer that came down in the Southwest with little alien guys.

"I was just in awe. . . . If something like this captures your imagination at that stage of life, you never get rid of it. It's in the blood." In time, Pflock would become an important UFO investigator.

Meanwhile, the "dead aliens" myth won backing from an unlikely source—Frank Scully, the Hollywood columnist for *Variety*. In 1950, Scully (whose prior scholarly works had included *Fun in Bed* and *Blessed Mother Goose*) wrote a book, *Behind the Flying Saucers*. According to Scully, his sources told him the saucers came from Venus. Their pilots were 3 feet high. A few saucers had crashed, killing aliens; the corpses were stored in secret government labs. A mysterious "Dr. Gee" told Scully about finding a landed saucer east of Aztec, New Mexico: "We took the little bodies out, and laid them on the ground. . . . The only trouble was that their skin seemed to be charred a very dark chocolate color." Scully's book was published by a distinguished house, Henry Holt and Co. A cheesy paperback edition followed. Its cover showed frightened, half-clad women gazing skyward at saucers.

True magazine soon exposed the Scully book as a hoax. But it was too late. The best UFO stories never die; they live forever, immune (like arguments over religion and sports) to the cleverest disproofs. Indeed, Scully's book is the granddaddy of today's "dead alien" stories, including Roswell.

The modern version of Roswell dates from a 1980 book, *The Roswell Incident*. The authors were Charles Berlitz (best known for his pseudo-scientific bestsellers about the "Bermuda Triangle" in the 1970s) and William Moore. Even the zany *Fate* magazine said *Roswell Incident* is "about as bad a book as could be written on a subject of such potential importance." No matter; the ball was rolling.

In 1984, a Los Angeles TV producer named Jaime Shandera claimed that he had received an odd package in the mail. It had no return address and contained undeveloped 35mm film. He developed the film. Lo and behold, the pictures showed what appeared to be top secret government memos! They bore dates from the late 1940s, and at least one well-known signature—that of President Harry Truman. The documents described the recovery of alien bodies at Roswell. It was all part of a secret government project called Majestic-12, or MJ-12. Why would anyone ship such documents to an obscure TV producer, as opposed to, say, the *New York Times*? Again, no matter; the ball rolled faster.

Tabloid newspapers got interested. "Witnesses" of the Roswell crash began to appear on TV talk shows. Hollywood producers started chatting about Roswell over lunch. Hey babe—want to do a treatment on this Roswell thing? The players began dealing the deals that would lead to *Independence Day* (which, as of April [1997], had earned $800 million worldwide) and its many profitable clones.

Meanwhile, the MJ-12 documents proved to be a hoax. Veteran UFO skeptic Philip Klass cited a number of internal flaws in the documents—for example, they designated dates using a non-military style. Even pro-UFO journals participated in the exposé. For example, the Chicago-based *International UFO Reporter* showed that the Truman signature had been photocopied from a real document, then transposed onto the fake memo.

Who faked the MJ-12 memos? The hoaxer has never been positively identified, although fingers have been pointed in various directions.

Again, no matter; the ball was rolling so fast now that no one in Hollywood or the TV industry cared any longer what had fallen on Roswell. Vast profits would soon fall on the entertainment industry, and that was all that mattered. The cameras rolled. As a result, a generation is now growing up on TV images in paranoid Roswell-related shows such as *Dark Skies* and *The X-Files*, which feature government officials more sinister than the worst fantasies of Timothy McVeigh [the convicted perpetrator of the 1995 Oklahoma City bombing]. The consequences for public attitudes toward government will be interesting to observe in, say, 20 years.

The best UFO stories never die; they live forever, immune (like arguments over religion and sports) to the cleverest disproofs.

Meanwhile, a mystery lingers: What was all that debris on Mac Brazel's ranch? This brings us back to Karl Pflock. By the early 1990s, he was a writer and UFO researcher in Placitas, N.M. In 1992, he investigated Roswell for a leading saucer group, the Fund for UFO Research, and summarized his findings in a 200-page monograph. His conclusion: The mysterious object wasn't a weather balloon. Instead, it was something much more fascinating—a true relic of the early Cold War.

At that time, just after World War II, American officials had desperately sought to answer one question: Was the Soviet Union covertly testing atomic bombs? They feared a sneak attack that could annihilate U.S. cities. To see what Stalin was up to, they launched a secret project, codenamed Mogul. Scientists developed a huge balloon, 650 feet high, that carried special microphones. At the right height, they theorized, the microphones could "hear" the rumble of an atomic blast thousands of miles away. In the late 1940s, they test-launched the balloon from New Mexico and other sites.

In UFOlogy, a new religion is being born.

Via some brilliant detective work, Pflock discovered that in June 1947, the Mogul balloon had crashed near Roswell. Its debris was what Brazel had discovered on his ranch. To conceal Project Mogul, the military had claimed the object was an ordinary weather balloon. That was a lie—a white lie, necessary to protect a program vital to national security. The Mogul-Roswell link was independently discovered by another researcher, Robert G. Todd of Ardmore, Pa.

After Todd and Pflock's exposés, Rep. Steven Schiff of New Mexico pressured the military to declassify the Mogul documents. They were finally released in 1994 and made the front page of the *New York Times*. Too late; *Independence Day* was on the road to production (not that it would have made a difference).

The Roswell exposé shook UFOlogy like an earthquake. About that time, the field was reeling from debates over alleged UFO abductions and other wackiness; the MJ-12 hoax had led to vicious name-calling; and true believers were disheartened to discover that a top Roswell investigator, Don Schmitt, had seriously misrepresented his professional background.

But Pflock and Todd's exposés were the showstopper. UFOlogists' resulting torment is revealed in letters to a UFO newsletter published by one of the grand old men of UFOlogy, James Moseley of Key West, Fla. "When we believe something for a long time, we become more and more committed to that idea," one heartbroken UFO buff wrote. "If evidence surfaces that disabuses the long-held notion, we resist this and try to continue believing. The UFO movement faces this problem with the long-held Roswell case falling apart. . . . Already we see UFO believers trying to save the 'alien bodies' part of the hypothetical Roswell scenario, by theorizing that there was another crash at about the same time. But in over 40 years of searching for 'alien bodies,' they seem to 'exist' only in the dim memory of what somebody allegedly heard someone else say, many years before."

Moseley is the Samuel Pepys of UFOlogy: His gossipy newsletter has chronicled the field's controversies and catfights for four decades. The Roswell debacle disgusted him. I spoke to him after the Heaven's Gate suicides, by which time he seemed to have given up all hope for UFOlogy: "You see enough of this, and you get more skeptical," he said. "I don't believe any of the (UFO) landings. I don't believe in Roswell. Certainly people are seeing things in the sky that we can't explain, but I don't think we have any proof (they are aliens)."

No UFOlogist sounds more bitter than Todd, though. In the early 1980s, he was director of research for Citizens Against UFO Secrecy. The group took the federal government to court to force it to reveal UFO documents.

"I started out convinced there was a (government UFO) coverup," Todd said during a phone call. "But after some 20 years, I see no credible evidence of it.

"My disenchantment with the UFO research field started with MJ-12, when it became painfully obvious that people were lying. UFO 're-searchers' were lying about MJ-12. And that pattern (of lying) has continued on into Roswell." As a result, "I guess I've grown up a little bit, and become more critical of people. (Now) I don't have a lot of faith in people, a lot of faith in their ability to recount their experiences accurately or honestly."

He sees "no convincing or compelling evidence" that saucers are alien. "I'm embarrassed to be associated with (UFOlogy) anyway. People are so credulous, it's embarrassing."

Is the UFO movement doomed, then?

In the mid-19th century, two young girls in upstate New York claimed to have psychic powers. The Fox sisters made national news. They toured the nation, demonstrating how they could relay "messages" from the psychic world by cracking their joints. Much applause was generated, much money was made. From their stunt emerged the 19th-century spiritualist movement, which revived hopes of eternal life in those whose faith had been shaken by Darwinism.

Late in the century, one Fox sister told the truth: It was all a hoax. They had cracked their joints, that's all. No matter; by then the spiritualist ball had rolled into a fair-sized business, with magazines and conventions and countless phony psychics catering to the countless legions of the gullible. To this day, spiritualism survives in slicker, higher-tech forms such as the Psychic Friends Network.

The guilty conscience of one Fox sister didn't kill the spiritualist movement; nor will the discrediting of Roswell kill UFOlogy. Like one's choice of religions or football teams, UFOlogy defies rational scrutiny. Its allure transcends logic. As Voltaire said about God, if UFOs didn't exist, then humans might feel compelled to invent them.

"UFOs are a seductive alternative for a lot of people who no longer have faith in anything." [Philosopher] George Santayana could have uttered those words, but he did not. The speaker was Steven Spielberg, commenting in a recent biography on his classic UFO film *Close Encounters of the Third Kind* (1977).

Spielberg is on to something, perhaps more than he appreciates. Consider the film's hero, played by Richard Dreyfuss. By the last reel, Dreyfuss has lost "everything" as bourgeois society defines it—his job, his family, his faith in the government. Like the followers of Heaven's Gate, who gave up their worldly possessions and emotional ties, he has only one thing left: the aliens, who escort him aboard their gigantic (and Freudianly named) Mother Ship. Back to the womb, as it were. Then they loft him to the stars, perhaps never to return.

Such cultural tea leaves hint where we're headed as the millennium looms. In UFOlogy, a new religion is being born, a religion built around the fantasy of alien visitors, a religion that may gradually replace the old, tired sects that no longer satisfy the hungry heart. True, many UFO-watchers dread the alleged alien influx: They imagine midnight kidnappings by, and involuntarily mergings of flesh with, bug-eyed monsters from the stars. But others hope for better; like the film's hero, they welcome the celestial visitors. That they are deluded is beside the point; the future may be theirs. In a century or two, the American West, the land of the seeker and the second chance, may host hundreds of their chapels, within which stained-glass images of bug-eyed visitors will gaze benevolently on the faithful.

10

Humans Are Not Being Abducted by Aliens

Robert T. Carroll

Robert T. Carroll, author of The Skeptic's Dictionary *and* Becoming a Critical Thinker, *is a professor of philosophy at Sacramento City College in California.*

The distance between the stars makes it highly improbable that extraterrestrial aliens, if they exist, are visiting Earth. The theory that such aliens are abducting and experimenting on humans is implausible and lacks credible supporting evidence. People who say they have been abducted are fantasy-prone in ways similar to religious mystics who claim to have seen visions. Others may suffer from psychiatric disorders or sleep disturbances.

There is a widespread, though erroneous, belief that alien beings have traveled to earth from some other planet and are doing reproductive experiments on a chosen few. Despite the incredible nature of this belief and a lack of credible supportive evidence, a cult has grown up around the belief in alien visitations and abductions.

According to the tenets of this cult, aliens crashed at Roswell, New Mexico, in 1947. The U.S. Government recovered the alien craft and its occupants, and has been secretly meeting with aliens ever since in a place known as Area 51. The rise in UFO sightings is due to the increase in alien activity on earth. The aliens are abducting people in larger numbers, are leaving other signs of their presence in the form of so-called crop circles, are involved in cattle mutilation, and occasionally provide revelations such as the Urantia Book to selected prophets. The support for these beliefs about aliens and UFOs consists mostly of speculation, fantasy, fraud, and unjustified inferences from questionable evidence and testimony. UFO devotees are also convinced that there is a government and mass media conspiracy to cover-up the alien activities, making it difficult for them to prove that the aliens have landed.

It is highly probable that there is life elsewhere in the universe and that some of that life is very intelligent. There is a high mathematical probability that among the trillions of stars in the billions of galaxies there are millions of planets in age and proximity to a star analogous to our Sun. The chances seem very good that on some of those planets life has evolved. It is true that until very recently [Jan. 1996], there has not been significant observational evidence that there is even one other planet outside our solar system. Nevertheless it seems highly unlikely that our part of the universe came about in a completely unique way. If so, there should be planets and moons and asteroids, etc., in all the galaxies and around many of the stars in those galaxies. The probability seems high, therefore, that there is intelligent life elsewhere in the universe, though it is possible that we are unique.

We should not forget, however, that the closest star (besides our Sun) is so far away from Earth that travel between the two would take more than a human lifetime. The fact that it takes our Sun about 200 million years to revolve once around the Milky Way gives one a glimpse of the perspective we have to take of interstellar travel. We are 500 light-seconds from the sun. The next nearest star to earth is 4.3 light-years away. That might sound close, but it is actually something like 23,000 billion miles away. Even traveling at one million miles an hour, it would take more than 2,500 years to get there. To get there in fifty years would require traveling at over one billion miles an hour for the entire trip. Despite the probability of intelligent life on other planets, any signal from any planet in the universe broadcast in any direction is unlikely to be in the path of another inhabited planet. It would be folly to explore space for intelligent life without knowing exactly where to go. Yet, waiting for a signal might require a wait longer than any life on any planet might last. Finally, if we do get a signal, the waves carrying that signal left hundreds or thousands of years earlier and by the time we tracked its source down, the sending planet may no longer be habitable or even exist.

Despite . . . a lack of credible supportive evidence, a cult has grown up around the belief in alien visitations and abductions.

Thus, while it is probable that there is intelligent life in the universe, traveling between solar systems in search of that life poses some serious obstacles. Such travelers would be gone for a very long time. We would need to keep people alive for hundreds or thousands of years. We would need equipment that can last for hundreds or thousands of years and be repaired or replaced in the depths of space. These are not impossible conditions, but they seem to be significant enough barriers to make interstellar and intergalactic space travel highly improbable. The one thing necessary for such travel that would not be difficult to provide would be people willing to make the trip. It would not be difficult to find many people who believe they could be put to sleep for a few hundred or thousand years and be awakened to look for life on some strange planet. They might even believe they could then gather information to bring back to Earth where they would be greeted with a ticker tape parade down the streets of whatever is left of New York City.

Despite the fact of the improbability of interplanetary travel, it is not impossible. Perhaps there are beings who can travel at very fast speeds and have the technology and the raw materials to build vessels that can travel at near the speed of light or greater. Have such beings come here to abduct people, rape and experiment on them? There have been many reports of abduction and sexual violation by creatures who are small and bald; are white, gray or green; have big craniums, small chins, large slanted eyes, and pointed or no ears. How does one explain the number of such claims and their similarity? The most reasonable explanation for the accounts being so similar is that they are based on the same movies, the same stories, the same television programs and the same comic strips.

Alien abduction stories

The alien abduction story that seems to have started the cult beliefs about alien visitation and experimentation is the Barney and Betty Hill story. The Hills claim to have been abducted by aliens on September 19, 1961. Barney claims the aliens took a sample of his sperm. Betty claims they stuck a needle in her belly button. She took people out to an alien landing spot, but only she could see the aliens and their craft. The Hills recalled most of their story under hypnosis a few years after the abduction. Barney Hill reported that the aliens had "wraparound eyes," a rather unusual feature. However, twelve days earlier an episode of "The Outer Limits" featured just such an alien being (Kottemeyer). According to Robert Sheaffer, "we can find all the major elements of contemporary UFO abductions in a 1930 comic adventure, *Buck Rogers in the 25th Century*."

The Hill's story has been repeated many times. There is a period of amnesia following the alleged encounter. There is then usually a session of hypnosis, counseling or psychotherapy during which comes the recollection of having been abducted and experimented on. The only variation in the abductees' stories is that some claim to have had implants put in them and many claim to have scars and marks on their bodies put there by aliens. All describe the aliens in much the same way.

Whitley Strieber, who has written several books about his alleged abductions, came to the realization he had been abducted by aliens after psychotherapy and hypnosis. Strieber claims that he saw aliens set his roof on fire. He says he has traveled to distant planets and back during the night. He wants us to believe that he and his family alone can see the aliens and their spacecraft while others see nothing. Strieber comes off as a very disturbed person, but one who really believes he sees and is being harassed by aliens. He describes his feelings precisely enough to warrant believing he was in a very agitated psychological state prior to his visitation by aliens. A person in this heightened state of anxiety will be prone to hysteria and be especially vulnerable to radically changing behavior or belief patterns. When Strieber was having an anxiety attack he consulted his analyst, Robert Klein, and Budd Hopkins, an alien abduction researcher. Then, under hypnosis, Strieber started recalling the horrible aliens and their visitations.

Hopkins demonstrated his sincerity and investigative incompetence on the public television program *Nova* ("Alien Abductions," first shown on February 27, 1996). The camera followed Hopkins through session after session with a very agitated, highly emotional "patient". Then *Nova* followed Hopkins to Florida where he cheerfully helped a visibly unstable mother inculcate in her children the belief that they had been abducted by aliens. In between more sessions with more of Hopkins' "patients", the viewer heard him repeatedly give plugs for his books and his reasons for showing no skepticism at all regarding the very bizarre claims he was eliciting from his "patients". Dr. Elizabeth Loftus was asked by *Nova* to evaluate Hopkins' method of "counseling" the children whose mother was encouraging them to believe they had been abducted by aliens. From the little that *Nova* showed us of Hopkins at work, it was apparent that Mr. Hopkins encouraged the creation of memories, though Hopkins claims he is uncovering repressed memories. Dr. Loftus noted that Hopkins did much encouraging of his "patients" to remember more details, as well as giving many verbal rewards when new details were brought forth. Dr. Loftus characterized the procedure as "risky" because we do not know what effect this "counseling" will have on the children. It seems we can safely predict one effect: they will grow up thinking they've been abducted by aliens. This belief will be so embedded in their memory that it will be difficult to get them to consider that the "experience" was planted by their mother and cultivated by alien enthusiasts like Hopkins.

The most reasonable explanation for the [alien abduction] accounts being so similar is that they are based on the same movies, the same stories, the same television programs.

Another alien enthusiast is Harvard psychiatrist Dr. John Mack, who has written books about his patients who claim to have been abducted by aliens. Many of Mack's patients have been referred to him by Hopkins. Dr. Mack claims that his psychiatric patients are not mentally ill (then why is he treating them?) and that he can think of no other explanation for their stories than that they are true. However, until the good doctor or one of his patients produces physical evidence that abductions have occurred, it seems more reasonable to believe that he and his patients are deluded or frauds. Of course, the good doctor can hide behind academic freedom and the doctor/patient privacy privilege. He can make all the claims he wants and refuse to back any of them up on the grounds that to do so would be to violate his patients' rights. He can then publish his stories and dare anyone to take away his academic freedom. He is in the position any con person would envy: he can lie without fear of being caught.

Dr. Mack also appeared on the *Nova* "Alien Abductions" program. He claimed that his patients are otherwise normal people, which is a debatable point if his patients are anything like Hopkins' patients who appeared on the program. Mack also claimed that his patients have nothing to gain by making up their incredible stories. For some reason it is often thought by intelligent people that only morons are deceived or deluded and that if a person's motives can be trusted then his or her testimony can be trusted, too. While it is true that we are justified in being skeptical of a person's testimony if she has something to gain by the testimony (such as fame or fortune), it is not true that we should trust any testimony given by a person who has nothing to gain by giving the testimony. An incompetent observer, a drunk or drugged observer, a mistaken observer, or a deluded observer should not be trusted, even if he is as pure as the mountain springs once were. The fact that a person is kind and decent and has nothing to gain by lying does not make him or her immune to error in the interpretation of their perceptions.

One thing Dr. Mack did not note is that his patients gain a lot of attention by being abductees. Furthermore, no mention was made of what he and Hopkins have to gain in fame and book sales by encouraging their clients to come up with more details of their "abductions". Mack received a $200,000 advance for his first book on alien abductions. Mack also benefits by publicizing and soliciting funds for his Center for Psychology and Social Change and his Program for Extraordinary Experience Research. Dr. Mack, by the way, is very impressed by the fact that his patients' stories are very similar. He also believes in auras and has indicated that he believes that some of his wife's gynecological problems may be due to aliens. Harvard keeps him on staff in the name of academic freedom.

Another contributor to the mythology of alien abductions is Robert Bigelow, a wealthy Las Vegas businessman who likes to use his money to support paranormal research and who partially financed a Roper survey on alien abductions. The survey did not directly ask its 5,947 respondents if they had been abducted by aliens. Instead it asked them if they had undergone any of the following experiences:

• *Waking up paralyzed with a sense of a strange person or presence or something else in the room.*

• *Experiencing a period of time of an hour or more, in which you were apparently lost, but you could not remember why, or where you had been.*

• *Seeing unusual lights or balls of light in a room without knowing what was causing them, or where they came from.*

• *Finding puzzling scars on your body and neither you nor anyone else remembering how you received them or where you got them.*

• *Feeling that you were actually flying through the air although you didn't know why or how.*

Saying yes to 4 of the 5 "symptoms" was taken as evidence of alien abduction. A sixty-two page report, with an introduction by John Mack, was mailed to some 100,000 psychiatrists, psychologists and other mental health professionals. The implication was that some 4 million Americans or some 100,000,000 earthlings have been abducted by aliens. As Carl Sagan wryly commented: "It's surprising more of the neighbors haven't noticed." The timing of the mailing was impeccable: shortly before the CBS-TV miniseries based on Strieber's *Intruders*.

Cultural delusions

Some of those who claim to have been abducted by aliens are probably frauds, some are very stressed, and some are probably suffering from a severe psychiatric disorder, but most seem to be fairly normal people who are especially fantasy prone. Most do not seem to be money grabbers, using their weird experiences as a chance to get on television or to have movies made of their lives. In other words, the testimony is often, if not mostly, made by reasonably normal people without known ulterior motives. If their claims were not so bizarre, it would be indecent to distrust many of them. Defenders of the reasonableness of belief in alien abductions point to the fact that not all of the stories can be accounted for by confabulation. However, hypnosis and other suggestive means are often used to access memories of abduction. Hypnosis is not only an unreliable method of gaining access to accurate memories, it is a method that can be very easily used to implant memories. Furthermore, it is known that people who believe they have been abducted by aliens are very fantasy prone. Being fantasy prone is not an abnormality, if abnormality is defined in terms of minority belief or behavior. The vast majority of humans are fantasy prone, otherwise they would not believe in God, angels, spirits, immortality, devils, ESP, Bigfoot, etc. A person can function "normally" in a million and one ways and hold the most irrational beliefs imaginable, as long as the irrational beliefs are culturally accepted delusions. Little effort is put forth to try to find out why people believe the religious stories they believe, for example, but when someone holds a view outside of the culture's accepted range of delusional phenomena, there seems to be a need to "explain" their beliefs.

Patients gain a lot of attention by being abductees.

Those who claim to have been abducted by aliens may be neither crazy nor telling the truth. It might be better to think of them as sharing a cultural delusion. They are similar to the people who have near-death experiences of going down the dark tunnel to the bright light, or who see Jesus beckoning to them. These shared experiences do not prove that the experiences were not fantasies. They are likely due to similar brain states in the near-death experience, and similar life experiences and death expectations. The alternatives are not either that they are totally crazy or that they really did die, go to another world, and return to life. There is a naturalistic explanation in terms of brain states and shared cultural beliefs.

Alien abductees might also be seen as similar to mystics. Both believe they have experienced something denied to the rest of us. The only evidence for their experience is their belief that it happened and the account they give of it. There is no other evidence. The comparison of abductees to mystics is not as farfetched as it might at first seem. The accounts of mystical experiences fall into two basic categories: the ecstatic and the contemplative. Each type of mysticism has its history of anecdotes and testimonials. Like the stories of abductees, the stories of each type of mystic are very similar. Ecstatic mystics tend to describe their indescribable experiences in terms clearly analogous to sexual ecstasy. Going from darkness into the light recalls the birth experience. The contemplative mystics describe their experience of perfect peace and bliss in ways which are reminiscent of a good night's sleep. In the more advanced stages of mysticism, the experience is clearly analogous to death: a state of total unity, i.e., no diversity, no change, no anything. In short, the fact that mystical experiences are described in similar ways by mystics born in different countries and in different centuries is not evidence of the authenticity of their experiences. The similarity speaks more to the uniformity of human experience. Every culture knows of birth, sex and death.

Abductees are very much analogous not only to mystics, but to medieval nuns who believed they'd been seduced by devils, to ancient Greek women who thought they'd had sex with animals, and to women who believed they were witches. The abductees' counselors and therapists are like the priests of old who do not challenge delusional beliefs, but encourage and nurture them. They do everything in their power to establish their stories as orthodox. It will be very hard to find an abductee who has not been heavily influenced in their belief by reading stories of aliens, or books like Strieber's *Communion* or *Intruders*, or by seeing movies featuring aliens. It will be even more difficult to find an abductee who has not been greatly encouraged in their delusion by a counselor like Hopkins or a therapist like Mack. Given a great deal of encouragement by a believing community, and reinforced by the high priests of the alien abduction cult, it is not very difficult to understand why there are so many people today who believe they have been abducted by aliens.

Yet, if there are beings clever enough to travel around the universe today, there probably were some equally intelligent beings who could have done so in ancient or medieval times. The delusions of the ancients and the medievals are not couched in terms of aliens and spacecraft because these are our century's creations. We can laugh at the idea of gods taking on the form of swans to seduce beautiful women, or of devils impregnating nuns, because they do not fit with our cultural prejudices and delusions. The ancients and medievals probably would have laughed at anyone who would have claimed to have been picked up by aliens from another planet for sex or reproductive surgery. The only reason anyone takes the abductees seriously today is because their delusions do not blatantly conflict with our cultural beliefs that intergalactic space travel is a real possibility and that it is highly probable that we are not the only inhabited planet in the universe. In other times, no one would have been able to take these claims seriously.

It is known that people who believe they have been abducted by aliens are very fantasy prone.

Of course, we should not rule out wishful thinking as being at work here. Although, it is a bit easier to understand why someone would wish to have a mystical experience than it is to grasp why anyone would want to be abducted by an alien. But the ease with which we accept that a person might want to have a mystical experience is related to our cultural prejudice in favor of belief in God and the desirability of union with God. The desire to transcend this life, to move to a higher plane, to leave this body, to be selected by a higher being for some special task . . . each of these can be seen in the desire to be abducted by aliens as easily as in the desire to be one with God or to have an out-of-body experience (OBE).

It is possible, too, that abductees may be describing similar hallucinations due to similar brain states, as [psychologist and author] Michael Persinger argues. Likewise, the ecstatic and contemplative accounts of mystics may be similar due to similar brain states associated with bodily detachment and a sense of transcendence. Using electrodes to stimulate specific parts of the brain, Persinger has duplicated the feelings of the sensed presence and other experiences associated with near-death-experiences (NDEs), OBEs, mystical experience and the alien abduction experience. The language and symbols of birth, sex and death may be nothing but analogues for brain states. Shared recollections of experiences do not prove that the experiences were not delusions. The experience which abductees think of as an alien abduction experience may be due to certain brain states. These states may be associated with sleep paralysis or other forms of sleep disturbances, including mild brain seizures. Sleep paralysis is a condition which occurs in that state just before a person drops off to sleep (the hypnagogic state) or just before they fully awaken from sleep (the hypnopompic state). The condition is characterized by being unable to move or speak. It is often associated with a feeling that there is some sort of presence, a feeling which often arouses fear but is also accompanied by an inability to cry out. The paralysis may last only a few seconds or longer. The description of the symptoms of sleep paralysis is very similar to the description many alien abductees give of what they remember experiencing. Sleep paralysis is thought by some to account for not only many alien abduction delusions, but also other delusions involving paranormal or supernatural experiences.

There are, of course, certain psychiatric disorders which are characterized by delusions. Many people with these disorders are treated with drugs which affect the production or functioning of neurotransmitters. The treatments are very successful in eliminating the delusions. Persinger has treated at least one person with anti-seizure medication which effectively stopped her from having recurring experiences of the type described by alien abductees and those with sleep paralysis. Countless schizophrenics and manic-depressives, when properly medicated, cease having delusions about God, Satan, the FBI, the CIA, and aliens.

No physical evidence

Even though the stories of alien abduction do not seem plausible, if there were physical evidence even the most hardened skeptic would have to take notice. Unfortunately, the only physical evidence that is offered is insubstantial. For example, so-called "ground scars" allegedly made by UFOs have been offered as proof that the aliens have landed. However, when scientists have examined these sites they have found them to be quite ordinary and the "scars" to be little more than fungus and other natural phenomena.

Many abductees point to various scars and "scoop marks" on their bodies as proof of abduction and experimentation. These marks are not extraordinary in any way and could be accounted for by quite ordinary injuries and experiences.

The most dramatic type of physical evidence would be the "implants" which many abductees claim the aliens have put up their noses or in various other parts of their anatomy. Budd Hopkins claims he has examined such an implant and has MRIs (magnetic resonance imaging) to prove numerous implant claims. When *Nova* put out an offer to abductees to have scientists analyze and evaluate any alleged implants, they did not get a single person willing to have their so-called implants tested or verified. So, of all the evidence for abduction, the physical evidence seems to be the weakest.

References

Baker, Robert. "The Aliens Among Us: Hypnotic Regression Revisited," *The Skeptical Inquirer*, Winter 1987–88.

Frazier, Kendrick. Editor, *The UFO Invasion: The Roswell Incident, Alien Abductions, and Government Coverups* (Buffalo, N.Y.: Prometheus Books, 1997).

Klass, Philip J. *UFO-Abductions: A Dangerous Game* (Buffalo, N.Y.: Prometheus Books, 1988).

Kottmeyer, Martin S. "Entirely Unpredisposed: the Cultural Background of UFO Abduction Reports," *Magonia* (January, 1960).

Loftus, Elizabeth. *The Myth of Repressed Memory* (New York: St. Martin's, 1994).

Persinger, Michael. *Neuropsychological Bases of God Beliefs* (New York: Praeger, 1987).

Persinger, Michael A. "Religious and mystical experiences as artifacts of temporal lobe function: A general hypothesis," Perceptual and Motor Skills, 1983, 57, 1255–1262.

Sagan, Carl. *The Demon-Haunted World—Science as a Candle in the Dark* (New York: Random House, 1995), ch. 4.

Sheaffer, Robert. "Unidentified Flying Objects (UFOs)", in *The Encyclopedia of the Paranormal* edited by Gordon Stein (Buffalo, N.Y.: Prometheus Books, 1996), pp. 767–777.

Sheaffer, Robert. *The UFO Verdict* (Buffalo, N.Y.: Prometheus Books, 1986).

11

UFO Sightings Are Products of the Unconscious Mind

Ronald D. Story

Ronald D. Story is the editor of The Encyclopedia of UFOs *and author of* Space-Gods Revealed *and* UFOs and the Limits of Science.

C.G. Jung, the famous Swiss psychiatrist, theorized that UFOs are a "living myth" that fill a void in people searching for spiritual meaning in their lives. UFO sightings and alien encounters can be seen as unconscious projections of human longings. Such yearnings can be exploited by unscrupulous people such as Marshall Applewhite, the leader of Heaven's Gate, a UFO cult whose members committed mass suicide in 1997. People should cultivate self-knowledge and not surrender control of their lives to others.

The great Swiss psychiatrist C.G. Jung (1875–1961) received a passing mention in the news, because some of his theories seemed relevant to the UFO cult Heaven's Gate. It is unfortunate that a mass suicide of 39 cult members is required to bring a moment's reflection on a topic of importance rarely dealt with in the media: the meaning of a human life.

As Erica Good stated in *U.S. News & World Report* (7 April 1997), Jung interpreted the UFO myth "as a projection of a higher self to which humans aspire." The very shape of the UFO—usually a disc or globe—reminded Jung of the mandala, or magic circle, which has been the universal symbol of order and perfection throughout the world since time immemorial. It also is the symbol of God and the higher self.

Speaking to the Basel Psychology Club in 1958, Jung said that although UFOs

> have always been observed, they didn't signify anything. Now, suddenly, they seem to portend something because that something has been projected on them—a hope, an expectation. What sort of expectation you can see from the literature: it is of course the expectation of a savior. But that is only one aspect. There is another aspect, a mythological one. The Ufo can be a *ship of death* [emphasis added], which

Reprinted from Ronald D. Story, "UFOs and the Meaning of Life," *The Quest*, Winter 1997, by permission of the author and the publisher, the Theosophical Society in America, PO Box 270, Wheaton, IL 60198-0270.

means that ships of death are coming to fetch the living or to bring souls. Either these souls will fall into birth, or many people are going to die and will be fetched by fleets of these ships of death. These are important archetypal ideas because they can also be predictions. If an atomic war were to break out, an infinite multitude of souls would be carried away from the earth. How one is to explain the Ufos in individual cases I cannot say. It depends on the circumstances, on a dream, or on the person concerned. There is indeed a void in individuals now that we are beginning to discover that our belief in metaphysical explanations has grown enfeebled. In the Middle Ages the Ufos would have been taken for divine manifestations, but we must say with [German writer Johann Wolfgang von] Goethe: "For all our wisdom, Tegel is still haunted." [*Jung Speaking* 390–91]

UFOs fill a void

In other words, even though our science has deposed the gods (including *the* God of the Bible), we retain the psychological need for them to exist and to intervene in our lives. UFOs and extraterrestrials fill in very well for the angels and demons that have been methodically erased from our world of scientifically respectable inhabitants. Nowadays, UFOs as space vehicles are accepted by at least half the population as a matter of course, and thus our vulnerability to those who would exploit such beliefs. As Jung reminded us elsewhere, "Man cannot stand a meaningless life" (*Jung Speaking* 439).

"About a third of my cases," Jung said, "are not suffering from any clinically definable neurosis, but from the senselessness and aimlessness of their lives. I should not object if this were called the general neurosis of our age" (*Practice* 41).

[French writer Albert] Camus once said: "I have seen many people die because life for them was not worth living. From this I conclude that the question of life's meaning is the most urgent question of all" (quoted by Jaffe). Jung thought that, in most cases, "A psychoneurosis must be understood, ultimately, as the suffering of a soul which has not discovered its meaning" (Jaffe 12).

UFOs and extraterrestrials fill in very well for the angels and demons that have been methodically erased from our world.

Although there are patterns to be discovered in nature, it is important to realize that what is called *the* meaning of life here is mostly our own personal meaning (or personal myth). It is not something to be discovered "out there," like a pot of gold at the end of a rainbow; it is the sense of purpose and significance that we find in, or assign to, our lives. We either find it or create it, and it becomes our reason for living.

What makes this so interesting—and dangerous, when caught unawares—is that our guiding myth operates mostly at the unconscious level. That is why Jung said, "One does not become enlightened by imagining figures of light, but by making the darkness conscious." Sometimes, only by studying our unconscious projections (as they appear symbolically in dreams and myths, works of art, hypnotic states, word association tests, etc.) do we discover our guiding myths.

Though not widely realized, myths are the stuff of life and we really do live by our myths. When a myth is put into practice, we have, in effect, created our own reality. That is what it means to be created in God's image; we are co-creators with God, containing within us latent powers which rarely reach their potential. As we can see from the example of Heaven's Gate, our myths can literally be a matter of life and death. The most important things to know are: (1) what myths we are living by, and (2) whether they are constructive or destructive. One of the best kept secrets in the world is how our personal myths can form the patterns of our lives without our conscious awareness.

The modern world

It is easy for us to speak of so-called "primitives," such as the Native Americans, for example, who having lost their myths also lost their meaning of life, with the result that their societies effectively disintegrated. What we haven't noticed, however, is that our own society—built more on pretense than substance—is undergoing a similar process. Despite what politicians have been telling us for the past century or so, the benefits of modern science have not produced the paradise-on-earth that was promised—not through the granting of material comfort for everyone nor through science's explanation of the mysteries of the universe—and it has certainly not given us the meaning of life. In fact, it has produced nearly the opposite effect: the more we explain the universe in scientific terms, the more pointless it becomes. But that is because science has left a key element out of the equation, namely, the human soul.

As my friend Lytle Robinson (186–7) once wrote: "The heart of the problem concerning the meaning and purpose of life, the key to the dilemma of 'Why are we here?' lies essentially in the existence or nonexistence of the human soul. If man has no divine spirit, then we are, *ipso facto,* no more than advanced animals, an evolved race of intelligent primates. Life would be without real meaning or lasting purpose. . . . Life would be much ado about nothing." He went on to say that humans are unique in the animal world because they possess ideals and a "compelling need to pay homage to a higher being." Robinson attributes this phenomenon to a "spark of the divine" within the human being, which could not exist were it not for our divine origin. "If man has a soul, a spirit, then he must be of spiritual origin, and there must be an origin—a universal force, being, or consciousness. There must be a God, for the created demands a creator." This was Jung's argument as well. And a corollary, I believe, is that if we are of divine creation, then we should not take lightly the destruction of that creation—self-destruction or otherwise.

Now, when you look around at the modern world we live in, we do seem like strangers on the earth. And it is precisely this phenomenon of *alienation* that makes the idea of extraterrestrials (and UFOs as alien ships) so compelling to so many people. According to Erich Fromm's definition (120), alienation is "a mode of experience in which the person experiences himself as an alien." Though it is possible that encounters with aliens could be taking place, it is my view that the term "alien" does not apply exclusively to extraterrestrials, but *applies to ourselves as well.*

In my view, the term "alien" is no accident. What I see happening is that we are seeing ourselves as aliens through a forecasting feature of our unconscious minds. In other words, through projection we are seeing ourselves as members of an alien society—an alien nation (as in "alienation")—that we fear will worsen if present trends continue. Put another way, the UFO-aliens are symbolic images of the *archetype of alienation:* a soulless sylph, who comes stealthily, like a thief in the night, to take away our humanity. This, in fact, was the real point of Jack Finney's 1953 science fiction classic *Invasion of the Body Snatchers*—stated clearly by the protagonist, Dr. Miles Binnell, when he said: "Sometimes I think we're refining all humanity out of our lives" (50).

The UFO-aliens are symbolic images of the archetype of alienation.

Whether it is the Big Brother of a corporation or the guru of a New Age cult, the point is the same. We are well advised to appeal to our inner resources first, and think for ourselves, before submitting blindly to others, who 99 times out of 100 do not have our best interests at heart. If we all had enough mutual respect for one another—as human souls, rather than human animals—the whole notion of following a guru would be unthinkable, especially if you consider that instead of following a benevolent God, you may be relinquishing your soul to the devil. How then do we help to change the mind-set that produced the [Heaven's Gate] tragedy at Rancho Santa Fe?

Two fallacies

The first step, I believe, is to recognize two closely related fallacies in thinking that help to keep those like Jim Jones and Marshall Applewhite in business. (The Rev. Jim Jones was the charismatic church leader who ordered the mass suicide of 914 followers in Guyana in 1978. Applewhite was the leader of the Heaven's Gate suicide cult.)

The first fallacy is that of *literalism.* Joseph Campbell said his favorite definition of religion is "a misinterpretation of mythology," which means "attributing historical references to symbols which properly are spiritual in their reference" (*Open Life* 78–79).

For Campbell, the meaning of idolatry is "mistaking the symbol for the reference" (*Business* 41). Myth is metaphor, in other words, a collection of analogies meant to be understood symbolically, not literally. Heaven, for example, is not a place—like some botanical garden on a perfect planet "out there" among the stars; it is what you create within yourself when you are reborn into a spiritual life. As Campbell often reminded us, the virgin birth is not about biology, and the Promised Land is not about real estate. The virgin birth symbolizes the birth of the spiritual life, as opposed to animal desires, and the Promised Land is the potentiality of that spiritual life within each of us. Which brings us to the second fallacy: seeking from outside what is obtainable only from within.

When asked about UFOs in an interview by Michael Toms on New Dimensions Radio, Campbell gave an answer that contained the essence of the concept of a God within. He said:

> I'm interested . . . in these theories that . . . the beginnings of many of our ancient civilizations are from visitors from outer space. I think this is a continuation of something that is at the core of our religious heritage, and I think it's not a very good aspect of our religious heritage; namely, that the spiritual power is from outside: it comes into us. God breathed his breath into dead earth. But the earth isn't dead. The earth is alive. Matter isn't dead; matter is alive. And matter is not anti-spiritual.
>
> . . . The spirit is not blown into man from without, but comes forth from the living of a noble heart; it's a quality of man himself.
>
> . . . If we get used to the idea the spirit comes from outside in, that the savior has come from elsewhere to us and is not a fulfillment of the potentialities of human life itself, then it may be that the fascination that more spirit, more messages, more truths, more wonders would come from outside; so that whether there are UFOs or not, the fascination with the UFO I regard as a continuation of this notion that the spirit and the giver of the spirit, and the power and the glory are "out there" somehow and not right here within us . . . that out there it would be somehow greater than here.

That also is why Campbell warned, earlier in the interview, against following a guru, but rather urged his listeners to trust in themselves. When submitting to a guru, he said, "the uniqueness of the individual is totally disregarded." This is antithetical to a philosophy of self-discovery and self-reliance. But the power of the self is difficult to comprehend if one is dominated by feelings of inferiority, inadequacy, and guilt.

Erich Fromm developed a theory to explain the phenomenon of Nazism in World War II, and totalitarian submission in general. What he came up with explains a great deal about why people join cults. In a nutshell, Fromm's theory is that people tend to "escape from freedom" because they fear it. They find freedom a burden too difficult to bear. And the main reason we fear freedom is that our society teaches dependence vs. independence. When we are put into a position of independence, we don't trust ourselves enough to feel up to the task.

Despite much lip service to the contrary, our society does not encourage critical thinking or individuality. (If there is money to be made from an original idea, that is perfectly acceptable, of course, but that is not the kind of individualism we are discussing here.) Now the tendency Fromm observed in a society that suppresses critical thought is to make one "an automaton . . . who loses the capacity for genuine and profound feeling and thought, and whose sense of identity depends on conformity" (quoted in Newman 380). No wonder we lose track of our identities. The bottom line is that, because of our social conditioning, real freedom makes us feel isolated and insignificant in a vast and lonely universe. When the Hebrew psalmist asked, "What is man, that thou art mindful of him?" this was but another form of the question, "What is the meaning of life?"

Rollo May (14–15) thought "the chief problem of people in the middle decade of the twentieth century is emptiness." He said, "By that I mean not only that many people do not know what they want; they often do not have any clear idea of what they feel." As one person put it, "I'm just a collection of mirrors, reflecting what everyone else expects of me." Inspired by a poem from T. S. Eliot entitled "The Hollow Men," May used the term "hollow people" to describe the feelings of powerlessness and emptiness that have become hallmarks of this age of anxiety.

In the case of the Heaven's Gate cult, guru Marshall Applewhite exploited these weaknesses to control his flock. He even had rules expressly forbidding the cult members to think for themselves. They were not to trust their own judgment or to use their own mind, according to a former disciple who left the cult in 1996.

Because Applewhite claimed to be the savior, his followers could shed the burden of freedom, believing that their guru and the benevolent space-gods would take care of them out of the kindness of their hearts and love for all humanoids in the galaxy.

A living myth

If this seems absurd, consider the fact that the same archetypal ideas have been drummed into us in Christian societies for two thousand years. What had previously been accepted as spiritual beings are now regarded as "technological angels" (in Jung's words), which are simply the gods of the age of science. As Richard Smoley, editor of *Gnosis,* has observed, "People have always seen the earth as inhabited by conscious beings other than ourselves," and "Today the mythic sensibility has been affected enough by science that people see those other intelligences as extraterrestrial" (quoted in *Newsweek,* 7 April 1997). When you add commonly accepted Christian themes to what appears to be space-age technology, for many the resulting mixture goes down without difficulty. Still, few people today realize the apocalyptic significance of the UFO phenomenon. Four decades ago, Jung tried to warn us. He said: "It is not presumption that drives me, but my conscience as a psychiatrist that bids me fulfil my duty and prepare those few who will hear me for coming events which are in accord with the end of an era." The UFOs, he said, "have become a *living myth.* We have here a golden opportunity of seeing how a legend is formed, and how in a difficult and dark time for humanity a miraculous tale grows up of an attempted intervention by extraterrestrial 'heavenly' powers—and this at the very time when human fantasy is seriously considering the possibility of space travel and of visiting . . . other planets." This tendency on the part of supposed extraterrestrials, he continued, "is a purely mythological conjecture, i.e., a projection," one that "was reserved for our enlightened, rationalistic age. The widespread fantasy about the destruction of the world at the end of the first millennium was metaphysical in origin and needed no Ufos in order to appear rational." But now that we live in the machine age, these omens take the form of a technological construction. Jung sums up the significance of UFOs in these two sentences: "The signs appear in the heavens so that everyone shall see them. They bid each of us remember his own soul and his own wholeness, because this is the answer the West should give to the danger of mass-mindedness." [Jung, *Flying Saucers* 16, 18, 78]

Few people today realize the apocalyptic significance of the UFO phenomenon.

Sir Laurens van der Post, Jung's biographer and long-time friend, quoted him as saying, "I cannot define for you what God is. I cannot tell you even *that* God is, but what I can say is that all my work has scientifically proved that the pattern of God exists in every man, and that this pattern has at its disposal the greatest transforming energies of which mankind is capable." This was Jung's own myth, which when brought to consciousness and actualized to the best of his ability, gave him the meaning of life.

Both Jung and Campbell taught that self-knowledge—which should result in self-confidence—and overall awareness are the keys to salvation. To say humans were created in God's image means that the higher self— the potential God within—is the god-image that we project into the heavens because we have not learned to believe in ourselves. The power of myth is the revelation that the gods of mythology are metaphorical representations of our own potentialities. Thus the power lies within us to create our own heaven or hell.

References

Campbell, Joseph. *An Open Life*. In conversation with Michael Toms. New York: Harper & Row, 1989.

———. *This Business of the Gods*. In conversation with Fraser Bos. Ontario, Canada: Windrose Films, 1989.

Finney, Jack. *Invasion of the Body Snatchers*. New York: Dell Books, 1978.

Fromm, Erich. *The Sane Society*. New York: Rinehart & Co., 1955.

Jaffe, Aniela. *The Myth of Meaning in the Work of C.G. Jung*. Zurich: Daimon, 1986.

Jung, C.G. *C.G. Jung Speaking*. Princeton, N.J.: Princeton University Press, 1977.

———. *Flying Saucers: A Modern Myth of Things Seen in the Skies*. Princeton, N.J.: Princeton University Press, 1978.

———. *The Practice of Psychotherapy*. Princeton, N.J.: Princeton University Press, 1966.

May, Rollo. *Man's Search for Himself*. New York: W.W. Norton & Co., 1953.

Newman, James R., ed. *What Is Science?* New York: Simon & Schuster, 1955.

Robinson, Lytle W. *Edgar Cayce's Story of the Origin and Destiny of Man*. New York: Berkley Books, 1976.

Organizations to Contact

The editors have compiled the following list of organizations concerned with the issues debated in this book. The descriptions are derived from materials provided by the organizations. All have publications or information available for interested readers. The list was compiled on the date of publication of the present volume; the information provided here may change. Be aware that many organizations take several weeks or longer to respond to inquiries, so allow as much time as possible.

Center for the Study of Extraterrestrial Intelligence (CSETI)
PO Box 265, Crozet, VA 22932-0265
(301) 249-3915
website: http://www.cseti.org

CSETI is a nonprofit research and educational organization that is dedicated to establishing peaceful and sustainable contact with extraterrestrial lifeforms. Its goal is to establish contact with and educate society about extraterrestrial intelligence. The center publishes numerous position papers and field reports on UFOs.

Citizens Against UFO Secrecy, Inc. (CAUS)
PO Box 20351, Sedona, AZ 86341-0351
(602) 818-8248
website: http://www.caus.org

CAUS is a nonprofit public interest group that believes that extraterrestrial intelligence is in contact with Earth and that there is a campaign of secrecy to conceal this knowledge. Its goals are to educate and enlighten the public about this cover-up and to fund further research into extraterrestrial contact with Earth.

Committee for the Scientific Investigation of Claims of the Paranormal (CSICOP)
PO Box 703, Amherst, NY 14226
(716) 636-1425 • fax: (716) 636-1733
e-mail: info@csicop.org • website: http://www.csicop.org

Established in 1976, the committee is a nonprofit scientific and educational organization that encourages the critical investigation of paranormal and fringe-science claims from a scientific point of view. It disseminates factual information about the results of such inquiries to the scientific community and the public. CSICOP publishes *Skeptical Inquirer* magazine, the children's book *Bringing UFOs Down to Earth*, and bibliographies of other published materials that examine claims of the paranormal.

Federal Bureau of Investigation (FBI)
Headquarters
J. Edgar Hoover Building
935 Pennsylvania Ave. NW, Washington, DC 20535-0001
(202) 324-3000
website: http://www.fbi.gov

The FBI hosts an official website that includes, among other things, an electronic reading room. The reading room offers all published FBI findings and articles on UFOs, with such topics as "Animal/Cattle Mutilation," and "Roswell."

J. Allen Hynek Center for UFO Studies (CUFOS)
2457 W. Peterson Ave., Chicago, IL 60659
(773) 271-3611
e-mail: infocenter@cufos.org • website: http://www.cufos.org

CUFOS is a nonprofit scientific organization dedicated to the continuing examination and analysis of the UFO phenomenon. The center acts as a clearinghouse for the reporting and researching of UFO experiences. It publishes the quarterly *International UFO Reporter*, the *Journal of UFO Studies*, monographs, and special reports.

National UFO Reporting Center
PO Box 45623, University Station, Seattle, WA 98145
UFO report Hot line: (206) 722-3000
website: http://www.ufocenter.com

Founded in 1974, the center serves as a headquarters for reporting possible UFO sightings. Such reports are recorded and disseminated for objective research and information purposes. The center maintains an on-line database of all reports and also publishes a monthly newsletter.

SETI League
PO Box 555, Little Ferry, NJ 07643
(201) 641-1770 • fax: (201) 641-1771
e-mail: info@setileague.org • website: http://www.setileague.org

The SETI League is a membership-supported, nonprofit educational and scientific organization dedicated to the search for extraterrestrial intelligence. Its publications include the books *Project Cyclops* and the *SETI League Technical Manual* as well as the quarterly newsletter *SearchLites*.

Skeptics Society
PO Box 338, Altadena, CA 91001
(818) 794-3119 • fax: (818) 794-1301
e-mail: skepticmag@aol.com • website: http://www.skeptic.com

The society is composed of scholars, scientists, and historians who promote the use of scientific methods to scrutinize such nonscientific beliefs as religion, superstition, mysticism, and New Age beliefs. It is devoted to the investigation of extraordinary claims and revolutionary ideas and to the promotion of science and critical thinking. The society publishes the quarterly *Skeptic Magazine*.

Society for Scientific Exploration (SSE)
PO Box 3818, Charlottesville, VA 22903
fax: (804) 924-4905
e-mail: sims@jse.com • website: http://www.jse.com

Affiliated with the University of Virginia's Department of Astronomy, the society seeks to provide a professional forum for presentations, criticisms, and debates concerning topics that are ignored or given inadequate study by mainstream academia. It strives to increase understanding of the factors that at present limit the scope of scientific inquiry. The society publishes the quarterlies *Journal of Scientific Exploration* and *Explorer*.

Ufomind
PO Box 81166, Las Vegas, NV 89103
(702) 227-1818 • fax: (702) 227-1816
website: http://www.ufomind.com

Ufomind hosts the world's most extensive website on UFOs and paranormal phenomena, and it seeks to provide a forum where all sides can be heard on these issues. The website houses a research index and a bookstore.

Bibliography

Books

Robert E. Bartholomew and George S. Howard — *UFOs & Alien Contact: Two Centuries of Mystery*. Amherst, NY: Prometheus Books, 1998.

C.D.B. Bryan — *Close Encounters of the Fourth Kind*. New York: Alfred A. Knopf, 1995.

Albert Budden — *Electric UFOs: Fireballs, Electromagnetics, and Abnormal States*. New York: Sterling, 1998.

Philip J. Corso with William J. Birnes — *The Day After Roswell*. New York: Pocket Books, 1997.

Roy Craig — *UFOs: An Insider's View of the Quest for Evidence*. Denton: University of North Texas Press, 1995.

Paul Devereux and Peter Brookesmith — *UFOs and Ufology: The First 50 Years*. New York: Facts On File, 1997.

Bill Fawcett — *Making Contact: A Serious Handbook for Locating and Communicating with Extraterrestrials*. New York: Morrow, 1997.

Michael Hesemann and Philip Mantle — *Beyond Roswell: The Alien Autopsy Film, Area 51, & the U.S. Government Coverup of UFOs*. London: Michael O'Mara Books, 1997.

Larry Kettelkamp — *ETs and UFOs: Are They Real?* New York: Morrow Junior Books, 1996.

Philip J. Klass — *The Real Roswell Crashed-Saucer Coverup*. Amherst, NY: Prometheus Books, 1997.

Kal K. Korff — *The Roswell UFO Crash: What They Don't Want You to Know*. Amherst, NY: Prometheus Books, 1997.

John E. Mack — *Abduction: Human Encounters with Aliens*. New York: Charles Scribner's Sons, 1994.

James McAndrew — *The Roswell Report: Case Closed*. Washington, DC: U.S. Government Printing Office, 1997.

Barry Parker — *Alien Life: The Search for Extraterrestrials and Beyond*. New York: Plenum Press, 1998.

Curtis Peebles — *Watch the Skies! A Chronicle of the Flying Saucer Myth*. Washington, DC: Smithsonian Institution Press, 1994.

Kevin D. Randle — *Project Blue Book Exposed*. New York: Marlowe, 1997.

Kevin D. Randle — *The Randle Report: UFOs in the '90s*. New York: M. Evans, 1997.

| Robert Sheaffer | *UFO Sightings: The Evidence*. Amherst, NY: Prometheus Books, 1998. |
| Elaine Showalter | *Hystories: Hysterical Epidemics and Modern Culture*. New York: Columbia University Press, 1997. |

Periodicals

Joseph Baneth Allen	"Flying Saucers: Is the Culprit Found?" *Final Frontier*, March/April 1997. Available from PO Box 16179, North Hollywood, CA 91615-6179.
Robert E. Bartholomew	"*Before* Roswell: The Meaning Behind the Crashed-UFO Myth," *Skeptical Inquirer*, May/June 1998.
Susan Blackmore	"Abduction by Aliens or Sleep Paralysis?" *Skeptical Inquirer*, May/June 1998.
Richard Boylan	"Inside Revelations on the UFO Cover-Up," *NEXUS*, April/May 1998. Available from PO Box 22034, Tulsa, OK 74121.
Thomas Carroll	"Dreamland," *Fate*, April 1996. Available from PO Box 64383, St. Paul, MN 55164-0383.
Hugh F. Cochrane	"High Strangeness from Within," *Fate*, July 1998.
Missy Daniels	"PW Interviews: John E. Mack," *Publishers Weekly*, April 18, 1994.
Julie Duin	"If the Truth Is out There, the Feds Aren't Telling," *Insight*, May 18, 1998. Available from PO Box 91022, Washington, DC 20090-1022.
Bernard D. Gildenberg and David E. Thomas	"Case Closed: Reflections on the 1997 Air Force Roswell Report," *Skeptical Inquirer*, May/June 1998.
James Gleick	"Abduction: Human Encounters with Aliens," *New Republic*, May 30, 1994.
Michelle Kelley Hardin	"Michigan: A Hotbed of UFO Activity," *Fate*, February 1996.
Irving Hexham and Karla Poewe	"UFO Religion," *Christian Century*, May 7, 1997.
Leon Jaroff	"Did Aliens Really Land?" *Time*, June 23, 1997.
Kal K. Korff	"What *Really* Happened at Roswell," *Skeptical Inquirer*, July/August 1997.
Thomas Kulp	"UFOs: A Demonic Conspiracy," *Fate*, April 1996.
Paul Kurtz	"UFO Mythology: The Escape to Oblivion," *Skeptical Inquirer*, July/August 1997.
Art Levine	"A Little Less Balance, Please," *U.S. News & World Report*, July 14, 1997.
Paul McLaughlin	"ET: The Extraterrestrial Therapist," *Saturday Night*, June 1995.
Christopher O'Brien	"Mutants and Mutilations," *Fate*, September 1995.

Omni   "The Roswell Declaration," October 1994.

Robert Sheaffer   "The Truth Is, They Never Were 'Saucers,'" *Skeptical Inquirer*, September/October 1997.

Dennis Stacy   "Cosmic Conspiracy: Six Decades of Government UFO Cover-Ups, Part 1," *Omni*, April 1994.

John Starr   "The Sighting," *Sky & Telescope*, May 1996.

Peter A. Sturrock et al. "Physical Evidence Related to UFO Reports," *Journal of Scientific Exploration*," vol. 12, no. 2, 1998. Available from PO Box 5848, Stanford, CA 94309-5848, or at http://www.jse.com.

Dave Thomas   "The Roswell Incident and Project Mogul," *Skeptical Inquirer*, July/August 1995.

Jacques Vallee   "Consciousness, Culture, and UFOs," *Noetic Sciences Review*, Winter 1995. Available from Institute of Noetic Sciences, 475 Gate Five Rd., Suite 300, Sausalito, CA 94965-0909.

Michael Warren   "A Rift in the UFO Ranks," *Final Frontier*, November/December 1996.

Jim Wilson   "Roswell Plus 50," *Popular Mechanics*, July 1997.

Jim Wilson   "The Secret CIA UFO Files," *Popular Mechanics*, November 1997.

Index

abduction by aliens, 7, 10, 16, 17, 21
  attention gained by claims of, 83, 84
  childhood memories of, 51
  cult-like belief in, 80, 85
    origins of, 81
  as cultural delusion, 84
  and healing, 52–53
  as illusion caused by sleep paralysis, 86
  inability to remember, 53–54
  is physical, not psychological, 55
  lack of evidence for, 79, 82, 86–87
  possible goals of, 56
Abductions: Human Encounters with Aliens
  (Mack), 10
Air Force, U.S., 7, 15, 23
  and alleged Roswell coverup, 12, 13
  and denial of involvement in UFO
    investigation, 15
  Project Blue Book, 20–21, 68, 69
    beginning of, 6
    closure of, 67
  Project Grudge, 20
  report on Roswell incident, 14
  report of UFO received by, 70
Air National Guard, 28
alien remains, 12, 34–35, 38, 74
  and autopsy, 37, 39, 45–46
Amalgamated Flying Saucer Clubs of
  America, 23
American Association of Electronic
  Voice Phenomena, 24
American Astronomical Society, 58
American Psychical Society, 18
Ancient Astronaut Society, 24
Anderson, Bruce R., 41
Apollo space missions, 49, 50
Applewhite, Marshall, 88, 91, 93
Arizona, 28, 39
Arnold, Kenneth, 6, 8, 19, 40, 41
Associated Press, 32
astronomy, 57–58
Atwater, P.M.H., 15–16
Aviation Week & Space Technology, 10, 71

Barnett, Grady L. "Barney", 31
Belgium, 47
  open investigation of UFOs in, 21
Berlitz, Charles, 75
Bigelow, Robert T., 23, 83
Binnell, Miles, 91
Bitzer, Barry, 15, 38

Blackman, Maggie, 23
Blanchard, William, 34
Blum, Howard, 13, 15
Book of the Damned (Fort), 19
Brazel, William "Mac", 34, 74, 75, 76
  rancher who found Roswell debris, 32
  held by military authorities, 36
Brethwaite, Chris W., 28
British Engineer Battalion, 45
Brookings Institution, 17
Brown, Harold, 20
Bryant, Larry W., 14

California, 21, 22, 28, 29
Campbell, Joseph, 91, 92, 94
Camus, Albert, 89
Carleton University study of UFO
  enthusiasts, 24
Carroll, Robert T., 79
Carter, Jimmy, 21, 38
Cascade Mountains incident, 6, 8, 19, 40
Center for Psychology and Social
  Change, 83
Center for UFO Studies (CUFOS), 18, 23,
  66, 67
Chatelain, Maurice, 50
Christian, David, 15
CIA (Central Intelligence Agency), 11,
  15, 22, 42
  created soon after Roswell incident, 40
  involved in alleged UFO coverups, 13,
    47, 73
  and research into paranormal
    techniques, 21, 61
Citizens Against UFO Secrecy, 14
Clark, Charles S., 9
Clark, Jerome, 55, 56
Close Encounters of the Third Kind (film),
  21, 77–78
Comet Hale-Bopp, 63, 72
Committee for the Scientific
  Investigation of Claims of the
  Paranormal (CSICOP), 14, 16, 24, 25
  hoaxes documented by, 11–12, 22
  skeptical approach of, 18
Communion (Strieber), 54, 85
Condon, Edward U., 21
Condon Report, 21
Congress, U.S., 14, 19, 20, 42
coverup of UFO investigations, 7, 12–13
  denied by government, 15, 19